WHEN HURT REMAINS

WHEN HURT REMAINS

Relational Perspectives on Therapeutic Failure

Edited by

Asaf Rolef Ben-Shahar and Rachel Shalit

Routledge
Taylor & Francis Group

LONDON AND NEW YORK

First published 2016 by
Karnac Books Ltd.

Published 2018 by Routledge
2 Park Square, Milton Park, Abingdon, Oxon OX14 4RN
711 Third Avenue, New York, NY 10017, USA

Routledge is an imprint of the Taylor & Francis Group, an informa business

British Library Cataloguing in Publication Data

A C.I.P. for this book is available from the British Library

    ISBN 9781782202073 (pbk)

Cover image: Bella (2014), Acrylic on canvas, by Lilac Abramsky-Arazi, www.facebook.com/dancelilac/

Edited, designed and produced by The Studio Publishing Services Ltd
www.publishingservicesuk.co.uk
e-mail: studio@publishingservicesuk.co.uk

CONTENTS

PART IV
AFFECTS ON THE EDGE

PART V
BROADER PERSPECTIVES

To Zohar and Shuy
Asaf

Dedicated to my loving family—Jossef, Matan, Nitzan and Ron,
and to all the daring souls—
those who seek self-awareness and growth
and those who dare taking this journey with them.
May your journey be blessed!
Rachel

ABOUT THE EDITORS AND CONTRIBUTORS

Julianne Appel-Opper, diplom-psychologist, psychological psychotherapist (German State licensed), registered Gestalt and Integrative psychotherapist with the United Kingdom Council for Psychotherapy (UKCP), MUKAHPP, supervisor (University of Birmingham, UK, accredited by the German Chamber of Psychotherapy). Since 2001 she has been a visiting tutor at psychotherapy training institutes in different countries. She has twenty-five years clinical experience. For twelve years she lived and worked in France, Israel, California, and from 1998 to 2006 in the UK. From 2006 she has been in private practice in Berlin. She has contributed to several journals and books about her approach "Relational Living Body Psychotherapy". She has offered conference workshops, lectures, and seminars in Berlin and internationally for many years. www.thelivingbody.de

Jessica Benjamin, PhD, is a psychoanalyst in private practice in NYC. She is a supervising faculty member of NYU postdoctoral psychology program in psychoanalysis and a co-founder of the Stephen Mitchell Center for Relational Studies. She is the author of three books: *The Bonds of Love* (1988), *Like Subjects, Love Objects* (1995), and *Shadow of the Other* (1998). Her forthcoming book is *Beyond Doer and Done To: Recognition Theory and Intersubjectivity in Psychoanalysis*.

Doris Brothers, PhD, is a co-founder of the Training and Research in Intersubjective Self Psychology Foundation (TRISP). She serves on the executive and advisory boards of the International Association of Psychoanalytic Self Psychology (IAPSP). She is co-editor with Roger Frie of the *International Journal of Psychoanalytic Self Psychology*, the IAPSP journal. The latest of her three books is *Toward a Psychology of Uncertainty: Trauma-Centered Psychoanalysis*, (2008). She is in private practice in Manhattan, New York, USA.

Muriel Dimen, PhD, is adjunct Clinical Professor of Psychology, New York University Postdoctoral Program in Psychotherapy and Psychoanalysis, and Professor Emerita of Anthropology, Lehman College (CUNY). On the faculties of many institutes, she is editor-in-chief of *Studies in Gender and Sexuality*; an associate editor of *Psychoanalytic Dialogues*; and a founder of the International Association for Psychoanalysis and Psychotherapy. Most recently, she edited *With Culture in Mind* (2011). Her *Sexuality, Intimacy, Power*, (2003), received the Goethe Award from the Canadian Psychological Association. She has also written *Surviving Sexual Contradictions*, (1986), and *The Anthropological Imagination*, (1977). Her co-edited books are *Gender in Psychoanalytic Space* with Virginia Goldner (2002); *Storms in Her Head* with Adrienne Harris (2001); and *Regional Variation in Modern Greece and Cyprus* with Ernestine Friedl (1976). She is a Fellow at the New York Institute for the Humanities at NYU, leads writing groups for psychoanalysts, and practices psychoanalysis in Manhattan.

Nancy Eichhorn, PhD, is a teacher/mentor, writer, and editor. She is the founding publisher and Editor-in-Chief of *Somatic Psychotherapy Today*, a co-editor for the *International Body Psychotherapy Journal*, an editorial assistant for *Body, Movement and Dance in Psychotherapy*, and a member of the European Association for Body Psychotherapy publications committee. Her writing résumé includes over 5,000 newspaper and magazine articles, and chapters in professional anthologies, including *About Relational Body Psychotherapy and The Body in Relationship: Self–Other–Society*. She is an avid hiker, kayaker, and overall outdoor enthusiast. Nature is her place of solace and inner expression.

Shai Epstein, EABP, is a registered body psychotherapist practicing in Israel and teaching in Israel and Europe. Shai co-founded the post-graduate relational body psychotherapy programme in Israel. He specialised in trauma-work, Raichen therapy, and in various modalities of body work. Shai is interested in altered states of consciousness and the connection between psychotherapy and politics, and he teaches these aspects. He has also written and published papers on these topics. Shai is married and a father to three children.

Elad Hadad co-founded the post-graduate relational body psychotherapy programme in Israel. He is an EABP registered body psychotherapist who specialises in trauma-work, and explores with small bodies (people) and bigger bodies (organisations, cultural settings) kinder and more vital ways of living and of being together. Integrating shamanic principles into his work, Elad brings spiritual awareness into his psychotherapeutic practice.

Offer Maurer, PhD, clinical psychologist, is the director of The New Wave in Psychotherapy Program at the Inter Disciplinary Center (IDC), Hertzeliya, and a co-founder of the Israeli Institute for Schema Therapy. The chairperson of the Israeli Association for Relational Psychoanalysis and Psychotherapy, he is also the founding director of the "Gay-Friendly Therapists Team", the first gay-friendly psychotherapy institute in Israel. Offer is a lecturer at The Centre for Academic Studies Or-Yehuda, and a guest lecturer in various international programmes on psychotherapy integration, LGBT issues, and Schema Therapy.

Shinar Pinkas, PhD(c), is principle and senior trainer at Psychosoma, the Post-Graduate Relational Body Psychotherapy School at the Israeli Centre for Body-Mind Medicine. She is a bibliotherapist, body psychotherapist, and supervisor in private practice. Her PhD dissertation (at Bar-Ilan University) explores the absence of the living body in psychoanalysis. Shinar lives in Israel with her partner and two lovely daughters.

Barbara Pizer, EdD, ABPP, is faculty, personal, and supervising analyst, and former board member, Massachusetts Institute for Psychoanalysis; assistant professor of psychology, Department of Psychiatry, Harvard Medical School; faculty and supervising analyst, Institute for Relational Psychoanalysis of Philadelphia; visiting faculty, Psychoanalytic Institute of Northern California; visiting faculty and member, Advisory Board, Toronto Institute for Contemporary Psychoanalysis; honorary member and faculty, Institute for Contemporary Psychoanalysis, Los Angeles; member, The Contemporary Freudian Society; member, International Psychoanalytical Association; associate editor of *Psychoanalytic Dialogues*; former board member, International Association for Relational Psychoanalysis and Psychotherapy; author of numerous articles on the analyst's disciplined and creative use of self; in private practice in Cambridge.

Stuart A. Pizer, PhD, ABPP, founding board member, faculty, supervising, and personal analyst, and former president, Massachusetts Institute for Psychoanalysis; assistant professor of Psychology, Department of Psychiatry, Harvard Medical School; faculty, supervising, and personal analyst, Institute for Relational Psychoanalysis of Philadelphia; visiting faculty and member, Advisory Board, Toronto Institute for Contemporary Psychoanalysis; honorary member and faculty, Institute for Contemporary Psychoanalysis, LA; member, The Contemporary Freudian Society; member, International Psychoanalytical Association; associate editor, *Psychoanalytic Dialogues*; associate editor, *The Psychoanalytic Quarterly*; past president, International Association for Relational Psychoanalysis and Psychotherapy; author of *Building Bridges: The Negotiation of Paradox in Psychoanalysis* (Analytic Press, 1998); he is in private practice, Cambridge, MA.

Asaf Rolef Ben-Shahar, PhD, Israeli psychotherapist, teacher, and writer. He founded two relational body psychotherapy programmes in Israel (Psychosoma) and the UK, and is regularly teaching worldwide. Asaf authored two books (*A Therapeutic Anatomy*, Pardes, 2013; *Touching the Relational Edge*, Karnac, 2014) and co-edited with Liron Lipkies and Noa Oster *Speaking of Bodies* (Karnac, forthcoming). He is the editor-in-chief of the *International Body Psychotherapy Journal*. Asaf is a father to two girls, a novice DJ, bird watcher, and loves dancing and hiking.

Joseph Schwartz, PhD, member of the Guild of Psychotherapists in private practice in London. His books include *Cassandra's Daughter: A History of Psychoanalysis in Europe and America* (Penguin and Karnac), and *Ritual Abuse and Mind Control: The Manipulation of Attachment Needs* (Karnac). He was guest editor of the *British Journal Of Psychotherapy* special issue, "Attachment: clinical, conceptual and historical themes (May, 2015).

Rachel Shalit, integrative and body-oriented psychotherapist, member of EABP and a former board member of the Israeli Body-Psychotherapy Association; member of Psychosoma, the post-graduate Relational Body Psychotherapy School in Israel. Her previous career specialised in learning organisations (continuous improvement and methodologies). This passion is now oriented to the psychotherapy field.

Matthias Wenke, MA, lives in Bonn, Germany. He is a counsellor & supervisor in Adlerian Individual Psychology (DGIP), has an MA in educational science, psychology, and sociology, and is a Healing Practitioner, yoga teacher, and author. He is a trainer and member of the Alfred Adler Institute North in Delmenhorst, Germany. He has trained in body psychotherapy with Asaf Rolef Ben-Shahar and Will Davis, trauma therapy (EMDR), client-centred counselling (Rogers), and others. www.praxis-individualpsychologie.de

Sharon Ziv Beiman, PhD, clinical psychologist, faculty Tel-Aviv-Jaffa College, Israel, co-manager of "Siach (Dialogue) Group—an Institute for Relational Psychotherapy", Tel Aviv, former chair of the Israeli Forum for Relational Psychoanalysis and Psychotherapy (the Israeli chapter of IARP), member of IARPP board of directors. Sharon has a private practice in Tel Aviv.

FOREWORD

Andrew Samuels

Well, the book, at least, is not a failure. Although no-one who has written or edited a book believes deep down that it is a "success" (whatever that might mean). Nor will it leave any lasting hurt or harm—quite the reverse. The book has a benevolent mission—to counsel, to advise, and to warn all clinicians. Candidates/trainees and students from all traditions will be only the more obvious beneficiaries because of the exceptionally wide range of contributions and the sensitive editorial structuring. I was troubled and inspired, rocked and confirmed, uncomprehending at times yet still believing I was getting it.

In 2001, in a book on politics, I suggested that a country like Britain should set up a National Failure Enquiry. The idea was based on what everyone in politics knows: that things do not succeed as planned, that all political careers end in failure, and that living in a "risk society" (Beck, 1992) means that we do not really know what the next problem is going to be. Interviewed on the radio, it was put to me that, as Britain's decline continues, the National Failure Enquiry would have to sit in continuous session.

An inquiry into failure

Much the same can be said about analysis, psychotherapy, and counselling (hereafter referred to as "therapy"). Reassuring noises about being "good-enough", or casting mere survival of the client as an achievement, do not alter the fact that, for the majority of therapists, there is some kind of ideal version of their professional selves in play (just as there is some ideal version of their personhood that often exerts a baleful influence). Phrases like "the therapy thought police" and "the supervisor on your shoulder" reveal how ubiquitous—and constipating—the ideal can be. But to announce blithely that one is not affected by it, can escape the pit with one mighty bound, is not credible. Hence, therapy as a profession, like politics, cannot only engage with failure as a regrettable but uncommon phenomenon. These human activities (politics, therapy) are comprised and fashioned by failure. Therapists can learn from politics, where struggle is the norm, how to move beyond over-certain accounts in which this (my policy, my treatment) is a success and this (your policy, your treatment) is a failure. Political dispute contests the binary on a daily basis.

Where are the colleagues?

Maybe it is just me, or my persecuted take on things, but I found myself wondering, reading these humane and ground-breaking accounts of failure, hurt, and harm in therapy work, where were the colleagues and the professional community or group in the mind of the therapist-writer. When shame is what is feared, it can often be located in what people say, or are imagined to say about us. Now, this is not all bad; group pressure is necessary if one is to do no harm. In workshops on motivation for choosing therapy as a career, it often turns out that the therapist-to-be is a highly aggressive individual. That is to say, going into this trade is often a way of managing such aggression and sadism. The interconnections between failure and shame, and between shame and the group, and between the group and the professional ideal, are lurking in the clinical stories presented to us here.

Here is an anecdote about a professional group ideal when failure comes into the picture. I occasionally work as a psychologist for a leading soccer club in London (in the Premier League). I gave a talk on "managing failure" (my usual *schtik*) and how managing failure is necessary to avoid disappointment. It was loosely based on Winnicott and "the analyst fails the patient but in the patient's own way". The players free associated to their frequent physical injuries (an occupational hazard) as a special kind of failure—in the eyes of the crowd as well as in the eyes of the team. The atmosphere was getting dangerously weepy when the chief sports psychologist held forth that "we don't do failure here, Prof!" This nipped in the bud a promising conversation in which the coaches had seemed to be learning something from the mainly young players about what was persecuting them from within.

Turning now to the wider question of doing no harm, I want to make two comments on features of the contemporary therapy scene (applicable in many countries, in my experience). The first concerns the image of therapy given on therapists' websites. The second concerns serious professional misconduct and boundary violations, including in the forbidden zone of sexuality.

I have made a small study of these websites, which in some countries are a major source of referrals for the practitioners. They are seductively calm places, with images of lakes, mountains, and stones, reassuring the seeker of therapy that he or she will be taken care of, that the work will proceed at the client's own pace, and that the client is someone with massive unrealised potentials that (only?) therapy can release. There is never any mention of how risky and dangerous therapy can be. Of course, it could be argued that this would put people off, and this is probably true. But is it not interesting how the public face of the profession, at least in this business of our websites, tells lies about how wild things are likely going to be when therapy is joined?

To press home the point, the mission of this book, which explicitly attempts to reach clients, could be said to be to speak the truth about the nature of therapy work. After all, surgery is painful, drugs have side effects, and too much exercise can overstrain a heart. I think that one reason the cosmetic version of therapy has taken hold so easily is that work in the area of the mother–child relationship (whether attachment or object relations in tone) is (has to be?) redolent of safety and security—holding seen as the ineluctable precursor of expanding one's horizons. But holding can limit those horizons, and sometimes taking risks is precisely what leads to the subsequent feeling of being contained. And the mother–child place is definitely not only a place of security and safety.

Sexual misconduct and other collective hurts

Now for the matter of sexual misconduct as a very specific boundary violation—and one that attracts a good deal of interest in formal and informal professional circles, and for all kinds of reasons. There was not a lot of attention paid in the chapters to boundary violations in the sexual area as serious failures in and of therapy, and as being one of the most active generators of lasting post-therapy hurt. As Muriel Dimen (Dimen & Amrhein, forthcoming) has cogently been arguing, the profession as a whole finds itself unable to manage these infractions, preferring to seek out and punish individual malefactors. Its group ethical sensibilities quail under the pressure for individual exceptions to be considered, empathic understandings of the therapist developed, and rehabilitative therapy be offered to him (and, sometimes, to her). We could discuss all that another time. What I want to do here is to flag up the ubiquitous and systemic failure and hurt constellated by sexual misconduct in particular (while not overlooking other boundary violations, for example to do with money, and holding people in treatment for far too long).

Many of the failures, hurts, and harms detailed in the book are further illumined if we take Dimen's perspective as paradigmatic: although therapy is a deeply personal and individual activity, its shadowy aspects may stem as well from its being a most dangerous method (in Sabina Spielrein's words, and she would know). Of course, this is also what phrases like "no gain without pain" are getting at, perhaps. The shadow is the thing we do not wish to be, and sexual misconduct is part of the professional shadow of therapy.

Naturally, boundary violations are not the only generalisable source of harm. Another that might be mentioned is the therapist's incorrigible desire to be right, to privilege his or her theory over the client's demurral or rejection of it. In his wonderful book, *The Analysand's Tale*, Robert Morley (2007) assembled accounts of therapy written by former clients of many of the great names in the field (mainly dead). One thing that struck me when reviewing the book was how often the therapy broke down because of what could only be described as an *argument* over theory. The therapist knew best! He or she does know, is not only supposed to know. I think that persisting with what one "knows" to be the truth when it is rejected by the client confronts a therapist with a difficult choice. He or she may decide to change tack. But can opinion, deeply held conviction, be so easily changed or abandoned? Should it be? Is it forbidden to be right in one's work as a therapist? Be that as it may, it seems it is hard to truly change one's mind. Jung said that every client needed not only a unique approach to the work, but also a completely new psychological system. But I do not think I would be howled down in Jungian circles for saying that he signally failed to follow his own desideratum here.

There is more to this business of the client saying "No". Part of being a therapist is to experience being told that you are useless, that the therapy is a washout, and the client is worse off than before. Accepting the client's verdict and not disputing it seems to be the professional default position—but, again, it is very hard to do it authentically. I have found myself on many occasions saying to a sympathetic colleague "But you should have seen him when he started!" Surviving attack is surely important, but there is an exquisite vulnerability on the part of the therapist when the client's boot goes in. We do not talk about this so much—client power. And client power is a positive thing too, when the client moves to make a more active contribution.

Mention of the therapist's vulnerability requires immediate mention of the therapist's power as a source of hurt, harm, and failure. Only one of the contributions to the book refers explicitly to the ineluctable power dynamics of the work itself, the client's sense (that many have reported) of being under the therapist's power and sway. Any account of the micro-politics of the therapy session brings these phenomena to light. When we consider the phenomenon of sexual misconduct and boundary violations, or reflect on the damage done by the therapist's maddening rectitude (as in Morley's book), we are in the area of specific abuses of power. Failures to negotiate power over a whole range of matters can lead to lasting hurt. I am thinking of apparently banal things like the setting of fees, scheduling of session times, holidays, and so forth. But, alongside such specific occurrences of power gone awry in individual instances, we have to think about this tendency as already built into the therapy project. Who knows, the fundamental power of the therapist may be what motorises growth, movement, insight. But it may not.

There is also the power of words to consider, and in this regard the book is, at times, revelatory, as the therapists struggle to formulate their contributions. In recent years, I have opened a small practice in accompanying and supporting therapists who respond to complaints about them from clients or colleagues. These respondents have lawyers provided by their professional indemnity insurance companies, and sometimes I am covered as well (but only sometimes). I see my role as offering a space for the respondent to reflect on how he or she has experienced being complained about, as well as to provide the lawyers with some insights from the point of view of a therapy professional. I do not offer therapy but invariably suggest that the respondent seeks it. Occasionally, if the respondent wishes to make a full confession and apology, I help with the process of that.

One thing I have noted when reading the complaints from clients is that the therapist is often depicted as using unacceptable words or phrasings to the client (actually, it is often about the client). The therapist makes an oracular, even a poetic, general comment about the client's character or personality that the therapist regarded as reasonable and benign and representing their intimate knowledge of their client. But, to the contrary, the client regards what their therapist said as a never to be forgiven slaughter of their core self. Yes, we could say it is a failure all right. The therapist consciously meant no harm but the client feels profoundly harmed. We could use a quotidian term and say, in understated vein, that there was a misunderstanding.

Just to give one example: the female client complained that the male therapist had stated that she was sexually unappealing. The therapist averred that what he had said was that the client rendered herself sexually appealing. Neither backed down and the therapist's apology or acknowledgement for hurting his client's feelings was not enough. Each had experienced the doer–done to dynamic that Jessica Benjamin writes about in her chapter in this book.

My experience of body psychotherapy (Reichian analysis), and my occasional practice of it, is that, paradoxically, there is less of a chance of misunderstandings like these. Maybe this is because anticipating misunderstanding still comes with the body psychotherapy territory. I would like to use the bully pulpit given to me to say that I do not think body psychotherapy carries with it specific risks of physical acting out. The practitioners are trained with this in mind. Is this something that verbal therapists might learn from?

Contexts of failure

So far, I have been more or less taking it for granted that when we say we have failed, or left hurt remaining, we not only mean it but regard it as inevitable. Is this as true as it seems to be? I remember one of my earliest supervisors handling my fear of doing harm by saying that she doubted I would ever be that effective! I think that there can be a grandiosity of anxiety here. It does not mean we should be blasé and put all our stress on a fantasy of destructiveness on the part of the therapist. But such fantasies are there, and they stem, perhaps, from the presence of aggression as a driver for choice of therapy as a career.

It was interesting, when doing some background reading for this Foreword, to encounter culturally diverse accounts of what constitutes success or failure in personal and social life. What might be considered as social or economic success in one culture may be considered as spiritual failure in another. I daresay cultural diversity is mirrored in considerable personal variation within a culture, dependent on life experience and on how "successful" one has been.

Drawing back the camera a bit further, I am wondering what the effect on clinical reflection on failure might be of the irresistible rise of the idea that there must be an evidence base for the provision and funding of any particular type of therapy. Randomised Controlled Trials, empirical work, and the scientific and academic approach to evaluating therapy all rest, if you think about it, on notions of failure and of success. Therapy must be "effective". A statistically effective therapy is a successful therapy. A therapy with no evidence base is a failing therapy. Managed care and the NHS should only pay for successful therapy (which, increasingly tendentiously, usually means CBT). Perhaps these developments, which all therapists know about, secretly influenced the conceiving of this book. Books do not exist in cultural or epistemological vacuums. Perhaps these collective policy manifestations are at work even in the individual practices of those whose professional set-up is independent, based on the payment of private fees. The high-end of therapy work may not be immune from the impact of audit culture and the measurement of everything as it imagines itself to be. No one is superior to economics.

Failure and the good-enough

I have been writing about failure and its relation to the good-enough for many years (Samuels, 1993, 1996, 2001, 2015) so it may not be an accident I was asked to contribute a Foreword. If it was an accident, then it was a synchronistic one. The way I would like to conclude is to share a few choice quotes on failure that have accompanied me. Sometimes, these words make me feel better; at other times, they fail to do so.

"Failure is the key to door to the kingdom." (Rumi)

"Every attempt is a wholly new start and a different kind of failure." (T. S. Eliot)

"Fail again . . . and fail better." (Samuel Beckett)

"There's no success like failure and failure's no success at all." (Bob Dylan)

London, October 2015

INTRODUCTION

Moshe Feldenkrais (1977), who developed the Feldenkrais method, considered walking as a series of controlled fallings. With each step we lose our balance and retrieve it. With each step we fall forward and block the fall with yet another step. Instead of perceiving falling as an undesired process, it becomes a prerequisite for moving forwards. Movement necessitates falling.

Similarly, when Steven Mitchell (2000) compared this to the analytic relationship he wrote:

> The analytic relationship is no longer usefully understood as the sterile operation theatre Freud believed it could be. The analytic relationship is not as different from other human relationships as Freud wanted it to be. In fact, the intersubjective engagement between patient and analyst has become increasingly understood as the very fulcrum of and vehicle for the deep characterological change psychoanalysis facilitates. (p. 125)

These two statements by Feldenkrais and Mitchell offer a position that is representative of attachment theory and relational thinking. Such a position is both hopeful and heavy. It is hopeful because it expects nothing more of the psychotherapist than being human. It is heavy because it expects nothing less. And human relationships are a messy business; they are saturated with hopes and expectations, with falls and rebalancing, desires and shame, hurt, fears, and needs. The more mutually involved we are, the deeper are the potential, and the risk, of the therapeutic encounter.

Many therapeutic relationships end with the gratitude and transformation of both parties involved; but since therapeutic relationships are not so different from other human relationships, many also end up painfully. As therapists, for most of the time we are left to carry that hurt on our own. At times, the pain and hurt can be processed in supervision and therapy, yet at others we carry it—secretly—for many years. Our vulnerability, which makes us suitable to practice, also makes us prone to take matters to heart, and it is not uncommon for us to bear the pain alone; secretly, shamefully.

Although failure, misattunement, and rupture are understood today as crucial to human development and inevitable or even necessary in the matrix of relating, as psychotherapists we still strive for, and often expect ourselves to refrain from failing, from making mistakes. At least some of this difficulty in accepting failures, working with these, and allowing them results from the "success culture" we grow in, where psychotherapy and relationships have become commercialised goods. Psychotherapists in training and at the beginning of their career are seldom taught how inevitable, or indeed how crucial, failure is. We are taught about attachment, about rupture and repair, but not about the pain of failing to help a client, about interventions that end up badly, clients who leave angry, clients we were simply unable to understand. Nor are we told of just how many times the therapeutic contact had not even reached the first session. Psychotherapy and psychoanalysis potentiate deeply involved relationships, we matter, they matter, which is a fertile ground for growth, and for pain.

The therapeutic walking can also be seen as a series of falls, ruptures, and repairs. When ruptures are repaired, these are no longer considered as failures, but as the basic tenets of therapeutic growth. Yet failure does exist, regularly so—and all therapists fail (Kottler & Carlson, 2003). Therapists fail at the beginning of their career, and they fail throughout it. It is upon these failures that novel steps are hopefully taken, that repairs occur, that experience is gained; it is upon these failures that we become psychotherapists, and manage to humbly and responsibly face the task of relating to others and supporting them through their suffering with our relatedness. Failure helps us in reorganising our self-agency beyond binaries of incompetence or omnipotence.

There are times where techniques take over the relationship, resulting in failed contact; other times where the therapist's specific orientation is limited and limiting the therapeutic scope. Sometimes therapy is simply ineffective, failing to meet the client's outcomes. As for the therapeutic relationship, while some therapeutic ruptures are repairable, we also have arguments and ruptures that can not be amended. We sometimes fail to help our clients; we often do not know what went wrong, and process our failures for many months or years. Some affects are too strong to handle, some enactments remain irreparable. Many therapeutic relationships do not reach closure at all, therapists are serially abandoned. Some falls do not end with another step.

This book is intended to tell the story of our failed attempts to connect, to help, to make a difference, with honour, and respect, and kindness. Our esteemed contributors share a repository of vignettes of things that did not work, of therapeutic mistakes, of empathic failures. Some of these failures saved therapy, while others marked the end of therapy. We sought to portray the human side of the clinical picture, when hurt remained.

In editing this book, we solicited papers that illustrated the myriad of ways in which hurt was created. Most papers involve a deep tear in the interpersonal alliance. We also wanted to show how this pain was understood and processed, but were less concerned with the analysis of failure (as nicely done by Goldberg, 2012). Sometimes processing failure or hurt was done within the therapeutic relationship. At other times, analysts or therapists had to process it on their own, and some of the papers in this book took years to process. While sometimes the pain remained bleeding for many years to come, it mostly also served as a call for introspection and growth. Perhaps we do not know how to grow without pain. We were deeply moved to witness how therapists carry their clients within their hearts for so many years, and with such heartbreak. If only clients knew how deeply they were cared for, how deeply they mattered. Perhaps, if some clients were exposed to their therapist's agony regarding the hurt they suffered, such knowledge would have brought transformation with it. We doubt that most clients realise the extent of their impact on the therapists who contributed to our book.

We chose to call this book *When Hurt Remains* since the cases presented here are those that were carved into the therapist's person, painfully so, and significantly impacted him or her. We are grateful to our authors who were willing to expose their personal and professional wounds, even though this was not always easy. This book will hopefully serve as an illustrative document of how human and vulnerable we are as people who choose psychotherapy as a profession. We truly wish to normalise, de-shame, and necessitate therapeutic failure as part of the learning process of becoming a psychotherapist by providing clinical examples and discussions by lead clinicians. For some writers, sharing their story was a healing act, and we hope that some aspects of this self-acceptance and healing would transmit to the readers too.

The overall orientation of this volume is relational, within which we present an integrative picture of relational psychotherapists working analytically, dynamically, and somatically with failures.

The book was written and edited with four groups of readers in mind: first, *trainee psychotherapists*: while we cannot learn from other people's mistakes, appreciating the complexity of the therapeutic relationship and the mistakes, failures, and pain therein can be a sobering and humbling support for training therapists, psychotherapists, and analysts at the beginning of their career. Second, *clinicians*: psychoanalysts and psychotherapists could enjoy the clinical material and benefit from discussions, illustrations, and different orientations and approaches to facing therapeutic failure. Third, *clients*: clients in psychotherapy might appreciate being exposed to some of the inner workings of psychotherapists, their thinking and feeling around mistakes and failures. Fourth and last, *intelligent lay readers*: people interested in psychology and psychotherapy would find this book interesting and inspiring.

We have divided the fifteen chapters of this book to five sections. Naturally, the themes of the sections overlap at times.

1. Beyond binaries: challenging binary thinking concerning success and failure.
2. Techniques: looking at the limitation of techniques and their relevance to failure.
3. Enactments: converging biographies and clashing self-states.

4. Affects on the edge: affect that is hard or impossible to process in therapy.
5. Broader perspectives: exploring contexts through which we can examine failure.

One last comment regarding confidentiality. Because of the content of the book, it was not possible to secure consent from all the clients. When such consent was not secured, biographical details were significantly altered to protect the client's confidentiality. Alternatively, some cases presented an amalgamation of clients, serving to illustrate a theoretical or clinical point.

Closing words

Editing this book helped both of us in developing a less dichotomous outlook on failure and success, and in realising the relativity of success and failure, and the contextual complexities of evaluating "good-enough" therapy. We saw how, at times, all the love in the world and all the efforts therein are still insufficient in preventing rupture and painful feelings for the client. Notwithstanding our responsibility to act good and do good, sometimes our therapeutic failures are exactly what he or she needed in their lives. And perhaps, as Stuart Pizer notes in his chapter, we are also called to let go of this very illusion—we frequently cannot know what our clients have taken from therapy, what was useful, and what created obstacles in their lives. We can only endeavour to do our very best.

PART I

BEYOND BINARIES

Introduction to Part I

Relational psychoanalysis hails from contextual thinking. Experiences should be examined under their socio–cultural, gendered, financial, and political contexts (among others). We aspire to move from either/or logic to both/and—to transcend binaries and discover thirds, thus retrieving the connection to previously dissociated aspects of ourselves and the other (Aron & Starr, 2013).

Can psychotherapy be accountable to binary concepts of success and failure? Can psychotherapy avoid it altogether and still remain sensitive to contextual changes? And if we do give up binary thinking of success and failure, how can we still maintain a system of personal and mutual responsibility, quality assurance of sorts?

The first section of this volume, *Beyond binaries*, examines some of the binaries in thinking of therapeutic success and failure.

Doris Brothers opens the section by challenging the polarity of success and failure, and points to their relativity and limitation. Jessica Benjamin conceptualises therapeutic positioning in case of failure, looking at the polarities of "good" and "bad" and, in particular, the challenge of the therapist to agree and bear "badness". Elad Hadad concludes the section with an uncertainty about success and failure in light of cultural indoctrination and expectation. He suggests that the perception of failure and success changes according to the perceiver, the angle of perception, and the scope of time.

CHAPTER ONE

Challenging the success–failure polarity in therapeutic practice

Doris Brothers

Who could doubt the wisdom of Rudyard Kipling's claim that being able to treat triumph and disaster—"those two imposters"—the same is a mark of maturity? Easier said than done, however, if you happen to make your living as a therapist! The siren call of the success–failure polarity seems to sound particularly sweet to our ears. Many published clinical vignettes read as if their authors, after struggling valiantly, had reached unequivocally successful outcomes; failures, if they are mentioned at all, are usually attributed to the patients' previous therapists. So widely shared is our delight in celebrating our therapeutic coups, and so great is our reluctance to let the world in on relationships that never get off the ground or land with a thud after a promising start (see Goldberg, 2012), that we rarely question the usefulness or validity of viewing our work as either successful or as a failure.

Judging therapeutic relationships as either triumphs or disasters has a long history. As far back as 1891, Sigmund Freud used the terms "success" and "failure" in relation to therapeutic practice. But even when the resolution of the Oedipus complex was the main criterion for judging the merit of an analysis, the determination of a treatment's success or failure was far from clear-cut. Those looking back with a postmodernist eye might ask by whose standards the criterion was met. The analyst's? The patient's? Was a consensus needed?

Aron and Starr (2013, p. 41) contend that psychoanalysis "has been hindered by its preoccupation with binaries . . .". The father of psychoanalysis himself modelled this preoccupation for us. I have conjectured that Freud's tendency to view psychological life in terms of such dualities as conscious–unconscious, primary process–secondary process, life instincts–death instincts, and masculinity–femininity, among many others, had self-restorative meanings for him. Biographies of Freud, as well as his personal correspondence, contain many references to his dissociative post-traumatic symptomatology. A number of likely traumas have been suggested, including the possibility that he was sexually abused by a nursemaid (Masson, 1985; Partridge, 2014). And there seems little doubt that he was deeply affected by the virulent anti-Semitism that pervaded his cultural surroundings (Aron & Starr, 2013).

The tendency to divide reality into dichotomous categories as a restorative effort in the aftermath of trauma is consistent with the theory I have been developing for some time (Brothers, 2008). In my view, trauma has two components:

1.   the destruction of the certainties that pattern psychological life that exposes its victims to the unbearable horror of self-annihilation, and
2.   attempts to restore a sense of certainty about what Winnicott (1965) calls our "going-on-being".

Insofar as feelings of uncertainty tend to be heightened by complexity and lessened by simplicity, either–or, dichotomous, thinking, which reduces complexity, is often a feature of restorative efforts in the aftermath of trauma. Thinking in terms of the success–failure binary may not always represent restorative efforts by therapists in the aftermath of trauma (although what therapist has not undergone trauma?), but it does provide a measure of relief as we engage in what must be one of the most complicated and therefore uncertain of professions.

I have little doubt that the way the success–failure binary is regarded depends, to a great extent, on one's theoretical orientation. Many postmodernists would recommend accepting the polarity's paradoxical and dialectical meanings; other relationally oriented analysts would suggest moving beyond it by conceptualising "the third". Still others, using a contextual perspective, would regard success and failure as aspects of experience that assume different shapes depending on their temporal, spatial, and relational contexts; not as opposing categories.

William James, the pragmatic philosopher, might have asked about the usefulness or "cash value" of the success–failure polarity. Its appeal seems apparent. Aside from appearing to bring a measure of perceived clarity to our highly uncertain profession, it promises to allow clinicians to learn from their own as well as others' mistakes and triumphs (Goldberg, 2012). And from the perspective of some psychoanalytic theories, notably self psychology, therapeutic gain hinges on the sequence of rupture (empathic failure) and repair (empathic success).

Why then am I questioning the usefulness of the success–failure polarity? When viewed from the relational systems perspective that I favour, the problems and complexities involved in thinking in terms of the success and failure of any given therapeutic relationship assume staggering proportions. Analysts' embedment within the interpenetrating systems that structure their relational worlds profoundly affects not only their understanding of what constitutes success and failure but also their experience of it. Adherents of one theoretical system may view as successful a treatment that would be viewed a failure in another. A horror of failure may be perpetuated in one analyst's cultural surround and family system but well tolerated in another. Just as the analyst's criteria for success and failure as well as his or her experiences undoubtedly affect a patient in countless ways, so too the patient's often unformulated criteria and experiences affect the analyst.

Another reason that I question the usefulness of the success–failure polarity involves the ways in which the duration of the treatment has been used as a criterion for judging the success or failure of a therapeutic relationship. I find that this criterion is often highly misleading. Many clinicians seem to believe that a therapeutic relationship should neither be too short nor too long, and that it should end after a suitable "termination" phase; the length of time considered optimal for any given therapy varies widely depending on one's preferred theoretical orientation. However, I can think of many exceptions to what may seem like sensible guidelines.

For example, a therapeutic relationship that ends quickly, say after only a few sessions, particularly when the patient is very young, may simply mean that a little has gone a long way. For patients who have never before felt that their needs and feelings deserved the full attention of another person, a brief therapeutic encounter that demonstrates that such attention is possible may in itself prove transformative. However, some therapies that last for decades seem to have more to do with a patient's compliance with the unspoken needs of his or her therapist than with any healing that is taking place. This is certainly an aspect of the clinical example I now present.

My Relationship with Lily

It was only after her analyst, Dr A, held a clock to her ear when the phone rang during a session that Lily reluctantly ended a five-day-a-week analysis that had lasted twenty-five years. In the weeks before this happened, the therapist had frequently phoned Lily at home, often sounding confused and distressed.

Lily phoned me on the recommendation of a relative's therapist, a colleague of mine. For the better part of the following year, our relationship was dominated by Lily's account of her complicated feelings about Dr A's precipitous cognitive decline and subsequent death, which she surmised was caused by Alzheimer's disease. She celebrated Dr A's keen intelligence and prestige in the psychoanalytic world as a writer and teacher, railed against her failure to acknowledge her impairment, and chastised herself for having abandoned Dr A in her "darkest hours". But hard as she tried, Lily seemed unable to reach any conclusion about the value of her long years with Dr A.

We agreed to meet three times a week for what I assumed would be a brief period of time. So urgent was her need to process her relationship with Dr A and its painful and shocking ending that finding out who I was or what a therapeutic relationship with me might offer rarely seemed to enter her mind.

Perhaps I can be forgiven for secretly comparing myself favourably to Dr A when I learned that Lily's relationship with her had long roiled with conflict. Dr A seems to have engaged Lily in a struggle about her connection to her parents, insisting that her inability to "separate" was the result of their severe pathology—and Lily's own. "Let them go," she would implore Lily. "You have me now." Lily confided that she had no intention of ever letting her parents go because she loved them dearly and they had loved her. Besides, she added, "I really didn't know what letting them go meant and Dr A never explained it to me in a way that made sense."

When, in the course of our work together, Lily and I realised that a familial trauma that occurred when she was only four years old had probably precipitated the depression suffered by both her parents, as well as the chaos that marked her growing up years, she was stunned. How was it possible, she asked, that after working with me for so long, Dr A had not recognised the significance of this tragic event? Lily also described her inability to write a novel, which was to have been a fictional rendering of the political scandal that brought shame and dishonour to her father, an official in local government. Dr A's repeated message had been, "Just do it. Sit down and write. You can take me with you." However, for Lily, sitting at her desk alone, to try to write was "torture". She apparently could not or would not take Dr A with her. We came to understand that at such times Lily re-experienced the terror that had so often overtaken her during the long lonely hours of her childhood. As her anger mounted over Dr A's failure to understand the many devastating effects of her childhood traumas, Lily's view of her long analysis became darker and darker. Eventually she declared that her analysis had been "a horrible failure".

It was not long after Dr A fell from the idealised position she had long occupied that Lily seemed to install me in this exalted role. She now made it clear that she regarded me as the embodiment of analytic perfection. She expressed no desire to set a date for ending therapy with me, and said she believed that her real analysis had only just begun. "You understand me so well," Lily would say reverently in response to what I regarded as fairly mundane utterances. She would ask for my help with simple quotidian decisions such as where and when to go on vacations and about what to serve at dinner parties, as well as more substantive ones including whether she should join a group for writers. She also became increasingly interested in me. Was I married? Did I have children? Where did I go to school? She seemed satisfied when I answered her questions as simply as I could without revealing information that I regarded as too personal.

If, during this period, I had been asked to bet on the outcome of our work together, I might have wagered that substantial healing was well within our reach, although, as you might imagine, I also anticipated that I would eventually fall in her estimation. Much self-psychological literature describes how a patient's disappointments in a therapist once seen as almost god-like in perfection contribute to the working through of "idealising transferences". I have found that when I am able to non-defensively acknowledge my "failures in empathic responsiveness", as they recommend, ruptures are usually quickly repaired. So I was not terribly surprised at Lily's initial bursts of irritation when flaws in my "perfect understanding" became evident. But I did not expect the intense rages with which she came to react to seemingly innocuous lapses in my attunement. For example, I once wished her a happy holiday after a session in which she had recalled painful scenes from her childhood. "Happy holiday?" she had howled, "how can you expect me to have a happy holiday after a session like this!"

As my attempts to acknowledge my errors in understanding fell on increasingly deaf ears, the happy ending I had hoped for now seemed all but unreachable. I worried that perhaps I was not the right therapist for Lily, that perhaps someone more like Dr A was who she needed. Yet I also felt it was important for me to stay the course. Then, one day, as Lily expressed intense outrage over some comment of mine that missed the mark for her, I was overcome with a feeling of deep sadness. Thinking about the poignancy of the feeling after the session, I recalled the sorrow I felt when my own analyst abruptly ended our twelve-year-long analytic relationship to relocate in a far away place. After my initial feelings of anger had subsided, I had been overcome with profound grief over my loss of a truly transformative therapeutic relationship.

Struck by the parallel between Lily's loss of Dr A and my loss of my own analyst, I suddenly understood why my previous interpretations had fallen flat. I had suggested that my lapses in empathic responsiveness recreated the world of her childhood in which none of her carers could be trusted to respond in reliably protective and guiding ways. However, I had not realised that my lapses in attunement reminded Lily of the devastating signs that Dr A was losing her mind. When I suggested that this might be true, Lily burst into tears. Her anguished cries filled several sessions. At last she was able to grieve her loss.

Just as I could recall how responsive and insightful my analyst had been once my anger at her had cooled, Lily's harsh condemnations of

Dr A gradually gave way to more positive recollections of the long years they spent together. Dr A, Lily now acknowledged, had helped her to gain confidence in her ability to think analytically, and had encouraged her interest in the classics and history; she had been very helpful when problems arose in her relationships with her children. But even more importantly, unlike her preoccupied parents, Dr A had demonstrated unwavering interest in Lily's life and had been reliably present in good times and bad.

Along with the growing integration of her perception of Dr A's unique strengths and weaknesses as an analyst was Lily's willingness to forgive my lapses in attuned responsiveness. After we had accomplished a great deal together, such as better understanding her tendency to take on the role of trustworthy carer for others as a way to compensate for deprivations in her own life, and after celebrating the progress she now was making on her novel, I had suggested that perhaps we could think about ending our therapeutic relationship. We had just begun to consider what this might mean for Lily when her husband was diagnosed with a life-threatening disease. We are now meeting once a week as Lily grapples with this tragic development. It is clearly not the time for us to end our work together.

I have long believed when a therapeutic relationship is truly healing, it enhances the therapist's development and well-being as well as the patient's (e.g., Brothers & Lewinberg, 1999). George Atwood (2011) uses the evocative term "radical engagement", to describe a psychotherapeutic dialogue by means of which the worlds of both partners are transformed. I would say that working with Lily has been transformative for me precisely because it has allowed me to confront my own struggles over success and failure. My early life, much like Lily's, was largely organised around the systemically emergent certainty, or SEC (Brothers, 2008), that my psychological survival depended upon meeting the emotional needs of my carers. Since I was convinced that my parents' well-being depended upon my excelling at all I attempted, I felt compelled to triumph in each activity I undertook.

Traumatic disappointments in my parents had transformed what might have been a context-sensitive certainty into a rigid, inflexible, certitude that gained new strength when I became a psychologist/psychoanalyst. If only I tried hard enough, I believed, I would enable my patients to achieve their therapeutic goals. This belief represented a restorative effort in the aftermath of my childhood traumas insofar as it enabled me to gain a measure of certainty that my "going-on-being" (Winnicott, 1965) was assured.

Although intellectually I understood that a patient's motivation to heal plays an important role in the unfolding of a therapeutic process, and that both the patient's and my participation in the relationship were greatly influenced by the multiple systems in which our lives were embedded, I nevertheless experienced each of my therapeutic relationships as if the outcome were entirely in my own hands. I would often sacrifice my own need for rest and restoration for what I imagined to be the good of my patients by working very long hours, taking calls at night and on weekends, and even making home visits on occasion.

While I had moderated these efforts to some extent by the time I began working with Lily, I was still driven by the sense that the success or failure of a therapeutic relationship depended solely on my own efforts. As is often the case with SECs, my understanding of the complex influences of the relational systems in which my relationships were embedded did not prevent me from feeling this way.

It was only after struggling to understand Lily's relationship with Dr A and the extreme shifts in her regard for me that I was struck by the harmful effects of my unconscious acceptance of the success–failure polarity. I had never before understood how forcing a therapeutic relationship into one or the other side of the success–failure binary obscured my appreciation of the rich complexities and inescapable uncertainties of the psychotherapeutic endeavour. Lily's ability to come to terms with Dr A's flaws and strengths as well as my own has served as a model for my own increasing ability to tolerate my experience of what has seemed like the unbearable uncertainties of my life.

In conclusion, I ask the reader to consider what it might be like to conduct a therapeutic relationship—and to write about it—without imposing the strictures of the success–failure polarity. Is it enough to hope that both therapist and patient will experience greater enjoyment in being alive for having engaged in a deeply meaningful human-to-human encounter that sometimes succeeds and sometimes fails to meet the expectations of both partners?

CHAPTER TWO

Enactment, acknowledgement, and the bearing of badness

Jessica Benjamin

I n this essay I will begin with the proposition that the developmental principle of rupture and repair (Tronick, 1989) corresponds with an essential relational clinical principle, namely the great therapeutic importance we assign to working through enactments. Against this background I will try to make some general comments about the analyst's role in enactments, and even more generally about the function of acknowledgment in relation to breakdowns. This perspective amplifies what I have previously written (Benjamin, 2004, 2009), about acknowledgment as an important aspect of recognition in the face of something we feel to be "failure". I wish to specifically address the aspect of breakdown that involves the analyst's subjectivity, her way of registering both the dyadic collapse into complementarity and her own contribution to it. I will stress the analyst's shame at failing and guilt at causing pain or shame as well as how truthful acknowledgment can make an essential contribution to the shared third and to reciprocal survival. I highlight the effect of the analyst taking responsibility for her contribution, as a way of formulating her insights into the mutual dynamic while simultaneously helping to regulate the affect of both members of the dyad. I believe the early rejections of discl
the psychoanalytic mainstream misidentified the issue by e

focusing on what the patient "finds out" about the analyst. Far more important are the explicit parsing of enactment, and the implicit regulation and soothing that occur when the analyst confirms by acknowledging the patient's perception. The confirmation, "this did happen", affirms the value of confronting and embracing a consensual reality and bearing together the painful truth (by no means a final or absolute truth)—a vital third.

How the therapist can or should use acknowledgment—whether or not it involves disclosure—relates to the two-person view of ruptures as well as to our understanding of the complementary structure. Complementary relations often lead to impasses based on flooding shame (Bromberg, 2006) in which a struggle is joined around blame: who is bad, crazy, difficult, who will own up (Russell, 1998).

As Russell, who considered such experiences unavoidable and called them "the crunch", first described, each partner is liable to feel, "Am I crazy or are you?" In effect, one person's mind has to be sacrificed for the other to live; the complementary structure of "submit or resist", as described by Ogden (1994a), allows for the validation of only one reality, one self. In such enactments the analyst's crisis may take the form of guilty, shameful awareness of being unable to avoid the complementary move of pushing the responsibility, that is blame, back into the patient.

Equally important, as Bromberg (2006) has noted, attempts at interpretation of what is going on—the analyst's effort to reach for the symbolic third—may appear as a dissociative move on the analyst's part. After all, the patient's conviction that the analyst does not want to know his dissociated self-state is based on the inaccessibility of a symbolic, differentiating third to that state.

In other words, unrecognised parts of the self do not "expect" to be known or part of a mutually accepting dialogue. They are covered in shame, hiding, and alone. The thing the patient is trying to get the analyst to know through enactment—the unconscious communication, as it were—inevitably involves a shameful part of the self, or one that is felt to be bad, and destructive of the other's love. Exposing this part can be excruciating, and so intensifies shame and disregulates the patient that even the analyst's effort to speak to the more symbolically organised "good patient" may thus appear as a wish not to know.

What follows from this dilemma, in my view, is that when the shame is great and the analyst is (unavoidably) unable to re-regulate the patient, she experiences her failure as a form of *harming*. The analyst's ensuing shame and guilt, her dysregulation, felt procedurally but left under cover of dissociation (Schore, 2003), may constitute a crucial element of repetition, of disruption in connection, for the patient. Frightened by our inevitable dissociation and dysregulation, we lose our contact with the basic principle of rupture and repair—and thus relive, along with the patient, the failure to survive breakdown.

In my experience, failures in self and other regulation and the reliving of breakdown, which activate the analyst's shame and guilt at harming, need to be countered by deep acceptance, by surrender to the third—here understood as the process of rupture and repair. This might be done by taking to heart Ferenczi's (1933) realisation that "it is an unavoidable task of the analyst, although he may behave as he will . . . take kindness . . . as far as he possibly can . . . will have to repeat with his own hands the act of murder previously perpetrated against the patient" (p. 52). The analyst's surrender to this inevitability becomes a way of restoring, strengthening, the third. The realisation might be phrased thus: the injury we find it unbearable to inflict, the wrong feeling we are pledged to avoid—returns in the form of enactment. Furthermore, it is often precisely by trying to avoid re-traumatising the patient that interactive knots are realised because we are then controlled by our fear of harm, failure, shame, and guilt. *That fate which we seek to avoid—as the Oedipus myth most importantly illustrates— meets us on the road to Thebes.* Believing he can escape destiny, and prevent inflicting the murder predicted by the oracle, Oedipus rushes to meet it. Expressing a similar notion, in the famous parable "Appointment in Samara", Death is informed by the master that his servant has fled because he feared meeting him in the market this morning, but Death replies he knows this, indeed, he has an appointment with the servant later that day whence he has fled, in Samara.

Ferenczi (1933) not only recognised the analyst's inevitable participation, but the patient's awareness of it (see Aron, 1996)—and hence the potential for mystification. Thus what differentiates the analyst from the original perpetrator is his willingness to acknowledge what was heretofore denied and take responsibility for his own difficulty in tolerating his response to the patient. This "willingness on our part to admit our mistakes and the honest endeavour to avoid them in future, all these go to create in the patient a confidence in the analyst" (Ferenczi, 1933, p. 33), and allow room for expression of critical feelings. He added, "It is this confidence that establishes the contrast between the present and the unbearable traumatogenic past . . . absolutely necessary for the patient . . . to re-experience the past no longer as hallucinatory reproduction but as an objective memory" (Ferenczi, 1933, p. 33). Only in this way can we break through the patient's loss of confidence in "the testimony of his own senses" and counter his identification with the aggressor—either of these we might consider as more likely to sponsor compliance in analysis than real reorganisation.

In this view, a significant aspect of retraumatisation is constituted by the analyst's failure to acknowledge, which the patient correctly grasps as the *avoidable* failure. It mystifies the patient in precisely the way she has been mystified as a child, and perpetuates the "doer–done" struggle. One likely outcome is that the analyst then feels accused, in effect "done-to" by the patient's suffering, which points the finger at the analyst's badness. When there is an underlying, if dissociated, sense that someone must bear the blame, the patient's insight can become a travesty of responsibility. Her observation becomes a simulacrum of the third, for it represents compliance to the other's demand, an unwilling repair of the other. In this way the complementary power struggle around blame may pervert the process of recognising responsibility, and the power to change self and other.

Historically, feelings of shame (by analysts of all persuasions, I suspect) have been sponsored by the long-prevalent ideal of being what, I suggest, could be called a "complete container". As opposed to accepting enactment, this ideal was built on the belief that one could avoid opening the patient's wound in the way Ferenczi saw as inevitable, that one could bring about rebirth without experiencing some form of "death". More concretely, the idea of the analyst's containing through insight and internal conversation the most difficult feelings without "leaking" implied that one could self-regulate in the face of the patient's hyperarousal without showing signs of struggle, without using communication to create mutual containment. Unfortunately, this expectation of sanity, so trenchantly critiqued by Racker (1968), seems to us relational analysts more likely to end in dissociation—denial of being affected. The alternative to this view is that the analyst exemplifies the internal struggle (Mitchell, 1997) and models the process of transcending failure as formulated by Slavin & Kriegman (1998) in their seminal paper "Why the analyst needs to change".

My argument here is not against the analyst using insight for self-regulation, but for recognising the limits of insight. Nor am I rejecting the idea that a patient will be stronger when she can take responsibility and be a contributor to understanding herself, the crucial relational theorem could be stated thus: expressing insight to the other is an *action*; it constitutes an acknowledgment of responsibility, not simply a fulcrum for a shift in the patient's self-awareness. When one person accepts responsibility for his actions it changes the other's view of him, and modulates the perception of the hurtful feeling; it creates a shift in self-state for the one who expresses the insight as well as the one who receives the expression. In the therapeutic dyad, insight should have meaning as an intersubjective act of communication, helping to create or reconstitute a shared third.

In complementary breakdowns the analyst might hold on to the belief that she is maintaining insight into the patient, that this constitutes a third in her own mind, even though she is no longer in empathic contact (see Feldman, discussed in Benjamin, 2004). It is precisely in this way that the analyst appears to be reproducing the original injury in the manner Ferenczi noted—for no matter how "kindly" and. educative the analyst may appear, she clearly thinks things have gone wrong because there is a wrongness in the patient. This refusal of the attribution or projection by the analyst in order to show the patient its true cause in his past paradoxically serves to re-enact that past in the present.

What is required on the analyst's part is actually the opposite: some kind of surrender and acceptance of who each of us is at that moment permits a relaxation of the tension—a step into the third—and thus allows another part of self to come on line. Observation may then feel more genuine and less defensive or persecutory. An invitation to join a shared third of looking together at "what has happened between us" may be procedurally more liberating than the attempt to figure it out for oneself, as Bromberg (Greif & Livingston, 2013) has noted.

Case example: from John Steiner

I wish to give an example from a most accomplished neo-Kleinian analyst of the difficulty that arises (or used to arise) when the analyst holds to the idea of regulating himself through insight and without acknowledging the two-way dynamic to the patient. My example, previously discussed in brief, comes from John Steiner's (1993) much studied article on analyst-centred interpretations, the article presented the view that the analyst should relieve the patient's anxiety (what we would call regulating) by showing understanding, by formulating what the patient must be experiencing as the analyst's action. While such relief through understanding might be necessary, Steiner argued, it was not itself curative; he insisted on the pre-eminent curative value of insight over being understood.

The vignette Steiner presents to make his case for understanding illustrates the dilemma of separating insight from acknowledgement, observation from intersubjective recognition. And let me add that I chose this illustration precisely because Steiner was in fact pushing the envelope in this paper, proposing that the analyst should use the help the patient gives by receiving patient's communications as corrective criticism of his work.

In the case vignette, Steiner reports a familiar interaction in which the analyst, who is struggling to contain the patient's projections, ends up pushing back into the patient by adding to his interpretation what he calls a second critical remark. He says this arose from his "difficulty in containing feelings . . . *anxiety about her and possibly my annoyance that she made me feel responsible, guilty, and helpless*" (1993, p. 144). Such analytic missteps reflect the common problem mentioned above, in which the analyst dissociates in the face of the dysregulation both partners are experiencing and becomes reactive, over-interpreting the patient. Steiner is not unaware of his difficulty containing, but what is he supposed to do about it in the moment? Note the usage *"she made me feel"*. Whenever we think in terms of someone "made me" do something, we are expressing the fact that we have moved into the doer–done to complementarity, a position characterised by inability to self-regulate. In effect, in that moment we have lost the space of thirdness where we can take responsibility rather than feeling something has been imposed. However, Steiner at this point does figure things out and tries to repair by using his self-awareness, reflecting on his countertransference. He makes an "analyst-centred" interpretation: he tells the patient, who by now has withdrawn, that *she* is afraid he "was too critical and defensive to understand her anger and disappointment . . . to recognize that she also wanted to make contact" (1993, p. 144). He goes so far as to add, using his countertransference to express his understanding, that she fears he "couldn't cope with these feelings because they would disturb MY mental equilibrium" (1993, p. 144).

However, Steiner did not actually admit to her that he *had* lost his equilibrium or minded having thereby hurt her, and he goes on to attribute her withdrawal in the moment not to his immediate comment but to her inability to reach him the day before. He stops just short of acknowledging that what she fears did come about, or that he is sorry for it. Or, we might say that he stops short of creating a shared thirdness, a space of reflection between them on what has actually happened.

Why, we might ask, is such a deftly containing formulation of the patient's fears not sufficient, why is stopping short of acknowledgment a problem? In part because Steiner's text goes on to detail how there has been a pervasive enactment with this patient, which takes the complementary form where each feels "the other is to blame". In other words, this struggle over blame appears to be the overriding relational dynamic that is unformulated, known but dissociated (Stern, 1997). Steiner reports in one passage that he generally has felt he was being made responsible for the patient's problems as well as his own, and in another reports the patient saying that he makes her alone "responsible for what happened between us" (Steiner, 1993, p. 144), and refuses "to examine his own contribution". Yet he does not note the symmetry—how his feeling about her mirrors hers toward him—and the two statements remain unlinked. What seems to be dissociated is the reciprocal nature of the dynamic, the ping-pong of blame, which might be halted by an action he explicitly does not permit himself—acknowledgment of his part; that is, he might break this deadlock by using what could be called—adapting his phrase—an "analyst-centred acknowledgment". It is at just this point in the narrative that he tellingly inserts an affirmation of his conviction that a "confession" is not advisable because it would only create more anxiety.

I would suggest that Steiner's ideal of "complete container" prohibits using the insights he shares with us and likewise prevents him from apologising to regulate himself and his patient. Indeed, at this point in the text Steiner reiterates the maxim that only patient-centred *insight into self* is mutative. Like him, it seems, the patient must make do with regulating herself through insight—awareness of her fear that he might not be able to contain her anger and disappointment, to recognise her need to connect. In fact, he has just shown us how he himself has actually failed to accomplish the feat of regulating self through insight. Whereupon I wondered: is it a remarkable reversal to demand this feat of the patient? Who will be made anxious, who will experience it as a failure if the analyst acknowledges fault? Is it too wild to ask if the patient's insight is introduced here *in the text where he speaks to us* because this is what re-regulates the analyst, restores his sense of function in role, his confidence in the third in his mind? Allows him to feel he can give the patient something and she chooses to make use of it? And, by the same token, is it not likely that the patient is restored to regulation because obliquely Steiner has admitted his fault, has acknowledged her fear of his failure to contain her anger? Is it not the insight and understanding of the other that helps the self to feel safe enough to restore connection and shift self-state?

Steiner (2006), many years later, reiterated his belief that such enactments, though unavoidable, are harmful to both the patient and the analysis. Harming remains an irreducible problem, but not one that can be ameliorated or made use of through acknowledgment. The problem this case exemplifies is not only that the analyst's dissociation will inevitably accompany the patient's, but that the analyst's inability to regulate in the face of the patient's helplessness will inevitably lead him to some subjective experience of being "done to". The patient's implicit or explicit accusation triggers the analyst's shame, and thus the patient's shame becomes the problem within the analyst, so to speak, for the analyst to be good (Davies, 2004). The danger of destructive fantasies has not been alleviated, only moved to the other side of the seesaw. Analyst and patient can still hurt one another. Rather than the safety of bearing this knowledge together we are left with dissociation as the protection against the fear of hurting and being hurt.

Paradoxically, the stance that is meant to protect the analytic container as a space open to all feelings good and bad—the stance of withholding direct acknowledgment of "what really happened"—may actually destroy the analytic function.

Acknowledgement and the failed witness

I would argue that the pressure exerted by an ideal of the analyst as a "complete container"—and by this I mean the unformulated belief that one who is unable to self-regulate without help is a shameful failure—potentially undermines the moral third and the analyst's witnessing function. The analyst is trying to protect the analytic role by masking personal vulnerability, yet in so doing fails as witness, exposing the patient to confusion and doubt about what is real, what is past, what is present. We then miss the opportunity to be both witnesser and acknowledger, re-instating the third by validating that some actions caused pain, felt like a violation of expectancy. This in turn causes fear that the third itself—the safety of responsible connection—could be lost.

In the process of focusing on his own regulation, the analyst is liable to dissociate from the extreme danger in which the patient finds herself, the choice between admitting to being destructive or being left alone without the safety of the attachment that part of her has counted on. That is, the analyst's own fear of harming becomes an impediment to recognising how frightened and destructive the patient might feel at this moment. Fear triggers a dissociation between those two alternating aspects, so that the "I make you feel bad" and "you make me feel bad" are unlinked, not held in a third position that witnesses.

Especially with severely traumatised patients, it is not a simple matter for the analyst to shoulder responsibility for hurting, because the patient's sense of danger, the patient's fear of being hurt by the analyst, is liable to overwhelm both partners. In the moment of enactment the symbolic equation between hurting and killing, the unconscious fantasies of destroying and being destroyed become powerfully active. I believe we have not fully realised a significant feature that appears when such fears of a dangerous object are enacted, especially for patients with a history of trauma or disorganised attachment. *There occurs an elision—a symbolic equation—between the analyst's apparent failure to witness and actually harming or abusing.* That is to say, many distressing moments are the result of the analyst having in some way dissociated the depth of the patient's fear and pain, rather than any directly injurious behaviour. Yet, it is hard for both partners to distinguish the failure in witnessing, from actually perpetrating the crime.

In such moments, to bear responsibility for the injury that is being re-enacted can appear both as an intolerable threat to the patient's safety and to one's identity as a reliable healer. (Tolerating threats to one's sense of goodness, as all analysts know, being one of the great challenges of our work.) At the same time, this failure cannot be denied because it would appear to be a denial of the original harm or abuse. In the moment, this can feel like an unresolvable paradox for the analyst. Yet it becomes all the more critical to find a way to acknowledge the failure in witnessing, not having fully taken in the depth of pain and terror, in order to gradually distinguish between failing to be fully present and actually denying or perpetuating abuse. The analyst needs to show the voice or face of the witness who is moved rather than that of the unmoved bystander upon whom the patient's suffering has no impact.

My question has been, how does the analyst bow gracefully to the inevitability that we must move through such moments of break-down, that healing without ever failing is an illusory goal? This takes us to the question of the analyst's surrender. I have suggested that we move beyond Ghent's (1990) powerful analysis of surrender by the patient to a view of the third as something that requires surrender by both members of the dyad, an asymmetrical but mutual process.

I do not wish to prescribe acknowledgment as a technique, rather show its role in renewing and building the moral third. I want to clar-ify that expecting the patient to contain or survive some knowledge of our failures is not necessarily asking the patient to tolerate failures without protest—it is precisely not asking her to hold the hot potato of blame, absorb all the badness in the relationship, not used to excul-pate the analyst or to extract forgiveness. It is rather suggesting that the notion of the third means that protest can be given a positive func-tion, that embracing the inevitability of failures prevents bigger fail-ures, and lets the analysis embody the principle of rupture and repair. This experience of thirdness offers the patient a different implicit model, a different interaction schema at the level of implicit knowing.

The ultimate aim of acknowledgment is therefore, of course, not to relieve the patient of the need for introspection, but to remove that process of gaining insight from a framework of blame and shame. It exemplifies the third thing: recognising that there are two participants who contributed to the interaction, and that the analyst is trying to see both at once as best she can. The analyst's act of acknowledging failure to hear, witness, or grasp the patient's experience helps to restore the third procedurally, then, even as it is often the first step in symbolically analysing the meaning of the enactment. Therapeutic acknowledge-ment is thus a highly nuanced action, undertaken to transform the complementary see-saw of blame into responsibility, invite the patient into a shared third, demystify, and free each partner to comment on what is happening. It is meant to show that the analyst *can* change (Slavin & Kriegman, 1998). It is an action that develops faith in the *moral third* because it affirms the lawful ethic of responsibility and counteracts past experiences of denial.

CHAPTER THREE

Life is no picnic

Elad Hadad

There is no doubt that the resistance of the conscious and unconscious
ego operates under the sway of the pleasure principle: it seeks to avoid
the unpleasure which would be produced by the liberation of the
repressed. *Our* efforts, on the other hand, are directed towards procur-
ing the toleration of that unpleasure by an appeal to the reality principle. (Freud, 1920g, p. 20)

My father is an alcoholic, the first born in a family of eleven
siblings. In his childhood he was the apple of his mother's
eyes, "*el aziz*" she called him, the prince. A symbol of
success, my father was the solid rock of the family.

From my early childhood I recall a handsome man, present, gentle,
and shy. I loved him and awaited his presence. I delighted in every
moment with him. When I was six, my grandma, his mum, died. My
father began to close down, increasingly withdrawing into himself,
losing his joy, and becoming a hurting and raging man, and later a
shadow of himself. I recall my childhood efforts to wait for him, to call
him back into life, to have fun . . . and my frequent disappointments.
I attempted to preserve his living presence even after months of not
witnessing it, and I remember the sense of guilt and failure for my

inability to "bring" dad back to life. To this day I feel my failure, and he is still alive; a shadow of himself.

This text will be confused, as I am in a confused space, feeling those secret hopes and beliefs powerfully clashing inside me, noting that I struggle to do what I am good at; a rebellion takes part in me: I do not want to work. I experience myself as standing by a locked door, behind which is *La dolce vita*, life that is easily lived, sensed, smelled, touched, a natural life, moist and fulfilling . . . while I, on the locked side of the door, powerfully sense the dryness, the desert, my cracked skin. It is the story of this nomad that I wish to bring here, his yearning—my yearning for water and my failure to quench my thirst. I succeed in helping others to adjust to a moist-less reality, to desert-like life, and my failure to help them in rebelling against this reality.

Danny, 1

Danny, thirty-eight years old, commenced therapy five years ago. Already, over the phone, he had approached me as a friend seeking advice and not as a professional, "I heard good things about you from someone I trust, and I need to clarify the edges. Can we sit together?" Two weeks later, as he entered my clinic, I saw a very handsome man, energetic, self-assured, and practical; yet also soft and personal in his manner. Danny sat and, with a charismatic smile, told me of his life.

He is a partner in a thriving, family owned, building company; he owns a house that he built with his own hands, and a few other properties. He is committed to his business yet manages to balance his professional and personal life, which he enjoys tremendously, "dropping the pen" at five-thirty every day. Danny regularly goes on holiday and, despite his managerial position, takes a month off every year. Danny describes his alone time, after work and on weekends and holidays as blissful, where he feels close to himself. He is loved and appreciated by everybody, family, friends, and customers, and by women. Danny had a few serious relationships, six weeks ago he ended the last one after two years.

As I listen, I note different parts in me responding to our conversation. I am impressed with him as a man, respecting his stature, his open yet humble sharing regarding his success. Danny is the type of man who evokes respect and appreciation in me. But what is he doing here? What is he asking of me? Danny responds with a composed narrative, wishing to look at a few conflicts in his life: his presence in the family business, his aspirations for freedom, and doubts regarding his capacity and desire for a partnership when he is clearly uninterested in having children. Towards the end of the session I notice a sense of being tested. What am I tested in? I wonder. "Have you seen other therapists?" I ask directly. "Yes," he replies, "a lovely psychologist, two days ago". "So how come you are here?" "I don't know," Danny answers, "she was empathetic and wise but something was missing." "You excited her, and she couldn't see the despair and loneliness in your eyes," I say. Silence. "Nobody does, I want to see you again," Danny responds after a few moments. It is easy for me to notice despair and loneliness.

My success and failure

Approaching the writing of this paper, I was pondering about the binary aspects of success and failure in my own life. To start with, my "life project" has succeeded. I survived, I held on, functioned, bore difficulties, challenges, and loneliness. I managed to contain aggression and sublimated my desire to cease from living in my body. Another success was helping others achieve similar goals, a somewhat heroic archetype: tolerating difficulty with dignity, the urge to wake up in the morning and charge forward, harnessing resources whenever needed.

The shadow of this success feels as the failure of my life, the failure to enjoy it. I fail to delight and feel gratitude. I feel that I need to do something, to work hard to deserve joy, and even then it is but a replacement of the true joy, it becomes satisfaction from success, a recognition and affirmation that replace the orgone pleasure (Reich, 1948, 1951, 1973)—which is bodily in nature, a sensory and immediate delight in my aliveness. This pleasure, basic and simple, is lost like Rapunzel in the ivory tower that I need to conquer to arrive at, overtaking the dragons of effort, habit, functioning, shame, and guilt, which accompany actions that carry pleasure without benefit to the other. For years I invested in being of value to the other, in supporting, assisting, and providing meaning to clients and students on their journeys. I can take temporary pleasure from new ideas, from learning innovating methods, from a successful interpretation or the intimate therapeutic relationship I partake in. Yet during the last months, for the first time in my life, I experience a shift in the status-quo of shame, a shift that feels like a crisis, but also as growing faith in the possibility of change. For the first time in my life these pleasures no longer suffice, and shame changes too. I am ashamed in my failure to enjoy my life, in my failure to take pleasure and satisfaction—as well as the shame from wanting this pleasure.

My first memory is about pain, heroism, and loneliness; the second is about pleasure, togetherness, and sponsorship. In the first I am nearly three, getting accidentally hit by a swing and cutting my chin. I remember an empty swing, the hospital corridors, and a huge syringe. In my memory I am there on my own; and I also recall pride and independence: I have conquered my pain. In the second memory, from about the same time, I rest with my grandmother in her bed after lunch. I enjoy our bodies touching, and I explore her body. I remember the game, the shared laughter, her gentle way of setting me boundaries, the softness and warmth. This was the only time in my childhood where bodily pleasure was allowed; I remember it with privilege, security, and shared closeness.

My body is a container for suffering, distress, and conflict. My body can carry terror, anxiety, aggression, and abuse and carry on, waking up in the morning and doing what it takes. My body can function in unspeakable conditions.

On the other hand I need delicious food, good wine, nature, and frequent sex. I need all those "lower" bodily pleasures in order to feel human. It is complex—I do not need them to exist, I need them to be. I can function well for days, weeks, and months when neither of these needs is met, yet something in me will wither, I will become serious and experience little vitality; few are the people around me who would notice the change.

Pleasure is dangerous; it connects with sudden loss, abandonment, a slamming of doors, guilt, and rage. I can therefore control my drives, hold them in my body, I can stop, calm down, shift my attention from my needs to those of the others. But I always want and need too, and have never given up the potential for pleasure, bodily and emotionally.

Danny, 2

After a period of working together we began experimenting with touch, mostly gentle touch in the centre of the chest. Danny's body is rigid and tender, delicate and dense; I sensed his gentleness and responded to it. Our work softened the external musculature (King, 2011; Totton & Edmonson, 2009) and emotions gradually surfaced, deep, sharp, and quiet pain, muted heartache and helplessness. These had little words. Slowly we learned to remain present with this pain in our relationship.

Danny knows how to take pleasure, but is mindful of its temporary nature. He manages to enjoy his body mainly during sex. Slowly we discover the void in Danny's psyche, his desire to cease from being, his pleasure of non-existence. Recognising it brings forth his existential question about bringing children into a world full of suffering and abuse. "Why should I commit to a relationship where I would experience power struggles, destruction of the other, misuse, and mutual hurt? I do not wish to know these parts of mine," he says while I insist on the gifts of connections. Danny looks at the world as a bridge, with the eyes of a hermit, engaging with minimum karma. I reflect his other yearning for connection, for involvement. Danny concurs yet the question is still burning in him. Why should he accept the social structures of wedding and kids? Why not allow himself to live softly and peacefully? These are real questions for him and me, and I find myself invested in inviting him into life, into involvement, relationships. Why am I so invested? Am I frightened to stay on my own? Perhaps I refuse to recognise my own desire to retire? Perhaps I need him to rectify my own choices? Or maybe I am inviting my bereaved father into life? I gently share with him my conflicts, and Danny smiles, "Yes, I notice that you care," he replies.

Reichian legacy

Life is no picnic. I heard this phrase time and again in my life. "Money doesn't grow on trees", " 'don't feel like it' stays at home", "nobody does just what they want". I grew up as an obedient child, doing what was needed, seemingly blending in, appearing mature for my age. I retained the belief that life could also be a picnic, pleasurable and delightful, yet it was hidden in the shadows, the fantasy, where it resided with its friends—excitement (including sexual), lust, desire, shame, and guilt.

It is sad to admit, but mostly I do not enjoy my work, which I believe I am quite good at. I can identify the components of suffering in the other (or perhaps they identify me), sense these in my body, recognising and reflecting them. I am unskilled in sharing joy with another, unpractised in being influenced by joy, generosity, and the love of others. Time and again I recognise fragility and vulnerability in the other, and my body organises around it. It is of value. I can meet my clients at the most abandoned and lonely places and offer them solace, containment, and connection. I can enjoy a successful moment in therapy but fail from enjoying the simple, bodily "orgiastic" pleasures (Reich, 1973) of life. As a therapist I am able to assist my clients in tolerating their inner reality when faced with painful life events. I can help them wait, suspend. But what about realities—inner and outer, which are worthy of changing; of being protested against? How come tolerating the reality is a higher value than the aspiration for delight, pleasure, joy, and satisfaction? Perhaps my addicted father and his surrender to satisfying his drives felt wrong. On the other hand, his alcoholism was a failed attempt to bear those circumstances against which he did not rebel (his relationship with my mother, for instance).

Body psychotherapy emerged as a protest against some Freudian psychoanalytic assumptions; from Reich's refusal to adapt, to accept Freud's withdrawal from working with the body and from cathartic work. Wilhelm Reich (1930, 1933) viewed societal oppression as a neurotic and dangerous attempt to control the spontaneous expression of emotion and drive (along with its overemphasis on cleanliness, confined sexual expressions, and eating etiquette). In my choice to practice body psychotherapy I have appointed Reich as my ancestor, yet my de facto clinical act is mostly guided by practices of adaptivity, sublimation, and holding back.

Danny, 3

As time goes by, our relationship deepens and Danny finds a partner. Questions keep arising and the fears, alongside his delight, of losing himself with her:

> outside the gushy river there is so much quietness and pleasure for me. Here, with Meital, I do enjoy and we share and I have a feeling of achievement and growth. I no longer disappear, but I also enjoy less; my fountain is not there.

I strengthen him, inviting him to find places of pleasant connection, to take pride in his containment of his desire to withdraw. Danny is proud, he is able to establish a relationship; he begins to think of children and marriage, yet doubt remains. Danny is honest with himself and Meital, taking his time to negotiate the next stage, as if this time is the only asset left for him, his honour. Danny is proud of himself but he is.not as calm, not as happy. He sees the price and wonders: "can I still save my soul?"

I went to his wedding. Danny got married and Meital got pregnant, and alongside the triumph; the good and happy moments, the strengthening and honest bond he created, Danny still wondered. A year ago we concluded therapy and in our last meeting Danny said:

> I love you. Without you this relationship wouldn't have happened. This marriage, my future—even the growth of my business. I have grown up but something in me feels defeated, I feel that I succumbed to comfortable choices and compromised my protest. I gave up protesting to social structures, to your love—you so wanted me to choose life and what it had to offer me. Have I really chosen? What was so wrong in staying out of the game? I was happy there, would you have helped me in attaining that too?

Epilogue

Concluding our work together, I was left with a sour sense of loss—of both success and failure. Was I but an agent of a society that idealises certain paths and roles (Illouz, 2008)? Have I colluded to make an unruly pact with Danny's superego and my own? Have I unwoven and diligently melted Danny's powers of resistance when faced with the Western linear flood of life, with evolutionary functionality? Have I abandoned Danny in his plea to withdraw, to refuse, to control his involvement, in his plea to be loved and accepted as a hermit?

Looking back, when I ask myself whether I helped my clients find more happiness, I am uncertain. I know that I helped them find quietness, peace, and acceptance, but is it enough? Giving up on neurotic and rebellious patterns can indeed contribute to a more mature personality, but do we not risk dulling the vitality, the shine, the edge? Could attaining the ability to live beyond the pleasure principle also be a marker of defeat?

Who said that life should be fun? Nobody promised me a rose garden? Why do I seek an opening to this closed door? Is it not merely an infantile wish to return to the womb, to paradise lost? Some people may argue that my chosen profession inherently requires staying with human suffering and pain (Bollas, 1986; Chodron, 1997). So what is the failure here?

I still carry an unyielding belief, deep within my cells, that we came here to experience pleasure. I believe that life, in its real essence, is a joy. And here, I feel that I have failed my duty as a psychotherapist—to honour the responsibility to enjoy and be awed by life and foster these, to sponsor the sensory and erotic delight from another's presence.

As for my father, perhaps alcoholism was his way of rebelling against societal schemas that created him, forcing him to position himself in certain ways. Perhaps it was his way of claiming his life back. Maybe there was a third beyond the binary choice (Aron & Starr, 2013), between being a family symbol with no free choice and the possibility of ruining this symbol along with ruining his own body, hopes, and life. Could another person supporting my father have given him that option? A therapist? Perhaps.

PART II

TECHNIQUES: HOLDING ON AND LETTING GO

Introduction to Part II

F amily therapist Carl Whitaker was known for saying that "techniques are things used while waiting for the therapist to show up" (Murray & Rotter, 2002, p. 204). This is, of course, part of the picture. Without technique, the psychotherapeutic act lacks rigour and structure. But techniques often become a convenient cathexis to attach to, sometimes on the expense of connection, or the ability to remain mindful of here-and-now occurrences. In attempting to balance science, art, and hermeneutics, mutuality and asymmetry, techniques can often turn from that which supports us and our work, to obstacles and hindrances.

In this section, three writers intimately share the hopes and pains around failure with technique. Stuart Pizer discusses enactive involvement and wonders about the possibility of foreseeing when to let go of therapeutic technique, illuminating the relational and mutual need to engage with surrender. Matthias Wenke portrays a painful collusive enactment of technique taking over the therapist and the therapeutic process. Finally, Shinar Pinkas tells her story as a client, a touching experience of a long-standing therapeutic relationship that was limited by a specific orientation. Her chapter points to the inevitable limitation of any singular orientation.

CHAPTER FOUR

"Put Down the Duckie": analytic vigour, rigour, and relinquishment*

Stuart A. Pizer

T his is a paper with a hole in the middle. I fell through that hole into the paper you are now reading. I begin with a back-story.

"Put down the duckie if you want to play the saxophone"

Rebecca (see S. A. Pizer, 2004), approaching the termination phase of her analysis, decided to give me a Christmas present. Knowing that my grandson, Ben, then two years old, was living in my house, Rebecca gave me a Sesame Street video titled "Put Down the Duckie". She told me it had been her favourite video to watch with her son, and she loved the idea of sharing it with me so that I could share it with my grandson. Among its many delights, its title segment is germane to this paper. In it, Ernie wants to join a cool jazz combo and play the saxophone. The problem is, he is determined to carry his rubber duckie and cannot bear to put it down. And, of course, clutching his duckie he cannot play the stops on the sax. So the very cool lead musician instructs Ernie that if he wants to join in and jam he has to put

*An earlier version of this paper was presented at an invited panel on "Vigour and Rigour", Division 39 Spring Meeting, New York, April 2005

37

down his duckie. This becomes a song, and several cameo guests—
including Jeremy Irons, Danny DeVito, Wynton Marsalis, Paul Simon,
Itzhak Perlman, Pete Seeger, and so on—join in the chorus with "You
gotta put down the duckie if you want to play the saxophone".
Rebecca commented that she was well aware of the transference rever-
berations in that song, and that giving me her gift was a loving way
of connecting with me while affirming her ultimate moving-on by
letting go of her analysis. As she commented, "I know I will have to
put down this duckie."

That is the back-story, one that I had not written into my original
paper about analytic vigour and rigour. That paper started out differently, as I will now share with you up to the edge of the hole that I
plunged through.

The paper prepared for presentation in 2005

A first glance at the terms *vigour* and *rigour* conjures a dichotomy. Are
vigour and rigour counterpoised? Some critics of the relational turn
contend that the analyst's exercise of vigour in the analytic process
constitutes an impingement—too much of the analyst, too much of the
analyst's stuff—all spillage into potential space, drenching the patient
in the analyst's otherness, foreclosing the freedom of association, of
autonomous mental functioning, of the patient's experience of alone-
ness in the analytic setting. From that particular vantage point, vigour
violates rigour; that is, when analytic *rigour* is defined in terms of a
technique based in abstinence, anonymity, non-disclosure, a disciplined adherence to empathic listening, and timely interpretation. Yet,
from another vantage point, rigour so defined represents the rigour
mortis of a stiffened, now defunct, version of psychoanalysis . . . a
familiar fossil "duckie" we may have difficulty relinquishing.

Enactive involvement—presenting the concept

What, then, may serve as a connective bridge that resolves the
dichotomy between psychoanalytic vigour and rigour? I choose the
bridge of *enactive involvement*. I believe that an involved, enactive
psychoanalytic technique is not an oxymoron, or a paradox, despite
the old injunction: "Don't just do something, sit there!" Aside from the

obvious fact that sitting there *is* doing something, I want to walk along the bridge of enactive involvement and consider how it may stand at the core of therapeutic—oops, I almost said *action*—and, although I feel love and gratitude for the wise and pivotal writings of Hans Loewald (1980) that have influenced me, I choose for now to use the term therapeutic *efficacy* (see White, 1963).

I want to say that at its core the efficacy of analysis is delivered in forms of enactive technique, perhaps reflecting the enactive mode at the basic, and embodied, levels of mental representation, prior to (and always underlying) iconic and symbolic modes of representation.

Contributions by others

Others have approached this psychoanalytic phenomenon: Ferenczi (1980) certainly experimented, generatively but sometimes quite misguidedly, with *active* methods; Hoffman (1998), of course, has explored the dialectic between ritual and spontaneity, or discipline and responsiveness, and he has noted that an enactment in analysis can later be interpreted like a dream to explicate its many tacit meanings; B. Pizer (2005) has described the analyst's offering of a poem or other form of what she terms a *Non-analytic Third*, some variety of *other-than-me-substance* that the patient may pick up and use, or not; Mitchell (2000) articulated the space between expressiveness and restraint; and Daniel Stern (2010) has written about analyst and patient as *partners in thought, a function both of witnessing and of finding together how to see the blind spots delivering reciprocal dissociative enactments.*

Focus on states in dyadic interaction increases enactive stance

As I see it, an enactive stance becomes a more evident aspect of our analytic repertoire as we shift our clinical attention somewhat away from an exclusive focus on mental contents and recognise the enormous importance of states, state transitions, state regulations, and dysregulations negotiated in dyadic interaction, and the force field of projective identification—or, to use a term I prefer, intersubjectivity—as a two person experience. This more *process* focus of analytic observation and intervention has been introduced in such contributions as Aron's (1996) papers on interpretation as the use of the analyst's subjectivity to alter the relational field; Mitchell's (1993) work on the negotiation of needs and wishes, and my own work on negotiation (S. A. Pizer, 1992, 1998, 2000, 2004, 2014); Beebe and Lachmann's (2002) writing on dyadic interaction; the neuro-psychoanalytic ideas of Allan Schore (2003); and Barbara Pizer's (1997, 2003, 2005) articles on disclosure and on the extrication of the analytic dyad from relational (k)nots.

In my original 2005 draft of this paper, I hoped to show how my enactive gesture of lending a patient the Sesame Street "Duckie" video advanced standard analytic work by opening fresh potential space, a shift in our relating, and key metaphors we could share to address issues of defence, affect, and relatedness.

Once having written that paper, I felt enthusiasm for the opportunity to illustrate how a spontaneous, improvisational analytic gesture helped allow for freshly discovered play in the analytic framework, in our emergent understandings, and in the patient's daily living. As I happily affirmed in my conclusion:

> Our analytic framework, as we know, can be our transitional object. In its rigour, our technique is always at risk of not keeping inside and outside sufficiently interrelated (to borrow a phrase from Winnicott), that is, to artificially distil the intrapsychic from the interactive relational field. Enactive vigour may at times facilitate, in a circular way, new potentials in the rigour of our analytic work. If technique is our "duckie", sometimes you have to put down the duckie if you want to play the saxophone!

Back to the clinical story: I should have known . . . should I have known?

Satisfying ending. But, you will notice, I have just skipped over the hole in the middle. What I skipped over is the clinical illustration, which I cannot now present to you. I had written about my work with a patient to whom, in a spontaneous expression of recognition, I had lent that video of "Put Down the Duckie". Indeed, this enactment proved to be strikingly useful in opening up realms of analytic exploration and emergent freedom both for my patient and the treatment process between us. So, in the glow of our enthusiasm that followed, I asked the patient for permission to write a draft of my paper, during my summer vacation, to be shared in the therapy—which he said he eagerly anticipated—for his response and possible consent. I was given an enthusiastic green light to write up our experience together, and so I did, carrying our shared work in my mind into my personal vacation space. After that vacation writing, I gave the patient my draft of that paper. And then the hole opened up and we tumbled through it.

My patient,[1] feeling accurately recognised in the narration of our clinical process together, nevertheless felt profoundly and traumatically *mis*recognised. Why? Because, he claimed, I wrote the paper in the first place.

We struggled through a month of meetings, twice a week, in which he berated me for what he called the devastation wrought by my paper. I should have known, he told me, that regardless of the prior permission granted to venture the writing of a draft *I never should have exposed him to a written account of our work.* I should have known him well enough to know that, regardless of his enthusiastic consent, he was someone never to use in such a way. I should have known that he needed to be shielded from exposure to anything written about him. He took this *breach* on my part to represent my clinical ineptitude, human insensitivity, and ethical failing. My inquiry, my apology, my assurances that I would not *use* him further by sharing our therapy process in the intended conference (or anywhere), failed to ameliorate his sense of betrayal, exploitation, and injury. We were each, in our own way, shocked. And we both, in our own way, tried to repair the breach. Paradoxically, I experienced that month of protest and mutual struggle as the most alive and intimately engaged time in our therapeutic process. But I could not take back my failure of empathic judgment, and its shocking effect on him, and we could not repair the breach. And my blithe narrative of a therapeutically invigorating enactment had morphed into another enactment: the writing and sharing of a paper that blasted a hole in our relationship. The ongoing therapy was lost in that hole.

Aftermath

The patient could not find his way back from disillusionment and distrust. And I was left to digest my raw experience of shame, frustration, and especially helplessness.

Could I have recognised that I was placing this therapy at excessive risk? Was I denying something, some predictive indications of his reaction? Why can't I find something now to say, some way to reconnect and repair this rupture? Is he refusing to let me succeed in my attempts to apologise and repair? Am I being too defensive to really get it? Have I committed an act of self-interest as a writer and thereby done irreparable harm as a therapist to this person?

I find it hard to bear the thought that my delight in writing the story of the "Duckie" video blinded me in some essential way.

I could do nothing that would manage to set our relationship *right* again. Although at moments I did feel like my patient was stubbornly refusing to let me make it right, or enjoy the fruits of our shared work, planting himself in a non-negotiable stand, ultimately I felt a primary responsibility for a rupture I was unable to repair. Inescapably, no amount of analytic vigour or rigour can protect a treatment from the unknown outcomes of each risk we take.

The patient, agreeing to consider seeking the consultation I urged and thanking me for the beneficial work we had thus far done, left and has not returned. He told me that I could never share the story of our therapy and how "Put Down the Duckie" had enlivened it, or impacted his life. However, he did grant that the ideas jacketing our story and the video itself still belong to me for my use. So this is a paper with a hole in the middle.

After thoughts—about writing on cases

Falling through this hole has been a chastening experience that leads me to reflect at other levels on what it means for the analyst to "put down the duckie". My presto riff on enactive technique must shift to a sadder adagio on relinquishment.

Perhaps the first relinquishment I must consider is the writing of my paper itself. A patient protests that I should have known never to write extensively about our work—at least, never to expose him to seeing a written account. Did I have the option of writing about this therapy with ample disguise but without the patient's consent? But I have never been able to tolerate the chafing feeling of keeping secret from a patient my use of any but the briefest disguised vignette. After all, what changes in the relational field when the analyst co-opts and exposes a patient's story with stealth? And what is unconsciously communicated right brain to right brain about the analyst's *secret*? We all know that the option of presenting or publishing without permission has been exercised many, many times—and we have all listened to or read such purloined stories. Is a certain dissociation deployed in the service of our professional field, our personal ambition, and our private needs to focus, formulate, and articulate the vast intersubjective experience in which we have been immersed in our consulting rooms?

A beloved colleague, Paul Russell (2006a,b), wrote stunningly about the truths of analytic process. Almost nothing of his was published in his lifetime, in large measure because Paul just would never write about his patients.

Do we relinquish clinical writing? No. I doubt that many of us would take that position. But what about the harm I did to *this* treatment? And could I have predicted it? How might I have seen beyond the ways some patients have said they benefited from my writing about them (see S. A. Pizer, 2000) to the ways this particular patient, and this treatment relationship, became piercingly disrupted?

I have not found the answers. Maybe that degree of prescience is essentially beyond us. Certainly beyond me. Beyond my blind spots. And yet, while committed to sustaining a reflective mindfulness, we must relinquish our illusions that we can predict or control therapeutic process. Which leads me to what else I must consider relinquishing.

In a sense, I believe the vigour and rigour of an analyst's work can be summed up as the relinquishment of what Harry Stack Sullivan (1953) called *security operations*, the constraints on experiencing and meaning-making that unwittingly insulate a person—in this case, the analyst—from mounting anxieties; that is, his "duckie" An analyst's security operations may lie in his relationship to standard technique, an adherence to the ritual that Hoffman (1998) has so cogently interrogated as a potential self-serving bunker for the analyst to remain hidden. Then again, the analyst's security operations may just as well entail a complacent assumption of his or her own pervasive good intentions and wholesome spontaneity. When we put down our duckies, we might also hold in mind that, paradoxically, even the playing of the most freely improvisational jazz is grounded in a deep musical structure.

Back to rigour/vigour—the analyst's "generous involvement"and
surrendering

Carrying within me the shadow of the therapy I ruptured, I have given much thought to the various benefits and risks of a more relationally involved mode of analytic work, and the attendant states of the analyst in this process. After all, rigorous *standard technique*, with its inflexible prohibitions, did provide a measure of protective formality. And, although a more generous involvement (S. A. Pizer, 2014) may take many forms within various psychoanalytic models—close attentiveness; empathic listening; holding the details of the patient's experience in memory; personal reverie within the analyst—the comparative informality and open-heartedness of a more mutually relational approach, with its intimate and expressive negotiations, may expose both patient and analyst to the intensified vulnerabilities of spontaneous interactive process, thereby complicating or thwarting the most disciplined practice of self-reflectiveness. The generously involved analyst struggles within the rigours of emergent shifts, continual uncertainty, surprise, emotional startle, and the precarious nature of clinical choices made amidst lived moments in an interactive field. And, in such relational hot zones, the delineating boundaries between the analyst's responsibility, his urgency, and his indulgence (as in believing that a written paper would be good for both analyst and patient) may approach a vanishing point. Those of us who believe in embracing a relational mode of analysis have experienced more clinical benefits than failures. But it thereby becomes especially incumbent on us to hold our intrinsic vulnerabilities with awe, humility, and a determination to face ourselves down as assiduously as possible within our inescapable limits of thinking whatever we are keeping unconsciously and defensively unthought.

In the midst of our surrender to generous and whole-hearted engagement, we rely on our ongoing practice of reflective self-inquiry and curiosity to awaken us from a soothingly stabilised dissociation. We rely on our accepting relinquishment of whatever has been helping us bear our surrender to the raw and destabilising vulnerability inherent in any deep analytic process, whatever within us is at risk of being held too tightly, or blindly. Analytic rigour requires this ongoing self-analytic, self-confronting, self-righting, and self-yielding process. We are always holding a duckie that blocks our playing all the available stops.

Relinquishment

Ultimately, my report of analytic vigour and rigour had to yield to a meditation on relinquishment. I had to relinquish a paper I liked about a treatment relationship that deeply engaged me. I had to relinquish my assumption that writing that paper and sharing it with that patient was a *good thing* to do, with potential to further the good connection fostered by the "Duckie" video. Once that paper broke our connection, I finally, sadly, had to relinquish my hope to find an adequate repair. I believe we all have to relinquish our conviction that writing about a patient will be good for that person, or bad for that person. We have to relinquish any illusion that our presuppositions have predictive powers. We have to relinquish self-reassuring assumptions that any amount of analytic vigour or rigour can protect a particular treatment from unknowable outcomes. We have to relinquish a tightly gripped adherence to any interpretive paradigm regarding transference or process. In one way or another, we just may have to relinquish our "Duckie" of the moment. And we have to relinquish the expectation that if we "put down the Duckie" the treatment cannot fail.

Note

1.   At this juncture, I need to say that I have been referring to this patient as just that, "this patient", in an effort to preserve total confidentiality. But this device also has the unwanted effect of conferring a formal and objectifying flavour to the person and to the genuine connection we had in our work.

CHAPTER FIVE

Technique as therapeutic escape

Matthias Wenke

Steven and Marina

S teven and Marina, a young couple in their twenties, want to marry in a few weeks. The session today is their second.

I originally counselled Steven who presented with panic, vertigo, nausea, and other psychosomatic symptoms, which turned out to be understandable as expressions of his deep fear of failure. With the support of breathing techniques and visualisations, we managed to stabilise these and he was able to reduce and later stop taking antipsychotics, prescribed by a psychiatrist.

Steven appeared reserved, shy, and almost speechless: I cautiously offered him possible descriptions of his state for him to accept or reject. It was a form of guessing game, where I provided myself as auxiliary ego for the unspoken in him.

It was noticeable when my suggestions touched him and were coherent. Those were precious moments where I often had the impression that he would rather hide again. In my spontaneous countertransference I realised an inner "redneck". Steven chose this name for one of his self-states, who liked to deny and crush out all soft or weak partial-selves, every vulnerable closeness, which he felt become embarrassing ("what is that for a sissy?"). The eye-contact was sparse; we scarcely looked at each other. As an infant, Steven feared exploring the world without his mother and was heavily undermined by his older brother. Together we discovered that his issue has been actualised by the impending lifelong choice for wife and family, which he experienced as an exam for his masculinity.

Steven and Marina have been together for about two years, the first six months went well, but then Steven's speechlessness and solipsism grew to a burdening extent. Marina complained of not getting any attention, saying there was not a single friendly word, and sometimes she felt almost disapproved of. He was totally self-absorbed and in the daily grind he did not talk to her. She wished that Steven changed this behaviour.

Steven acknowledged his inability to show affection. For him it was sufficient if his partner was simply around. In his childhood home a friendly language did not exist. He could not "escape my shadow", he said, remaining like a hedgehog. He wished to understand the cause and then leave this attitude behind.

Two of his inner credos were: "A man does not express love" and "One has to be cool". I imagine him as sitting blocked in a cage of discouragement and unrealisable expectations of masculinity, silent in his disruptive misery.

The problem of lacking attention has already been the topic of the last couple session, and when asked what they brought today they both replied: "The same as last time". I felt disappointed, that sounded like an accusation: "You haven't changed anything yet!" I have unconsciously taken over the responsibility of the expert, expected to provide a solution, and I felt overwhelmed with setting this deadlocked situation in motion.

The partners rarely made eye-contact with one another, but they did look at me. I could hardly stand their expectant eyes. I felt that I should have made his problem disappear; yet I was unable to identify this as countertransference or give it words.

I feel attracted to Marina, and I realise the threat of responsive countertransference as collusion with her to solve the problem of her partner. That would become humiliating, particularly as Steven has shared his jealous fantasies of a better man.

I feel disorientated, do not know where to start, where to grasp anything, I feel dizzy (one of Steven's symptoms) and powerless like in our previous couple session.

Attempting to escape helplessness

With this background I strongly wanted to approach this foggy and complex melange systematically and step-by-step. That was at least my rationalisation. I wanted to be well prepared this time, even though my entire counselling experience proved the opposite, that is, that the best is to plunge into each session spontaneously.

But I have not been convinced deeply enough by that, and furthermore I wanted to work in a methodical way. Thus I have planned for this session a very structured method from NLP (neuro-linguistic programming), the *Perceptual Positions* (Andreas & Andreas, 1991), so that I can draw on and follow the manual step-by-step.

From the outset I had a subtle feeling of self-deception, but it was not strong enough for me to drop my plan. Thus I offered both partners the opportunity to engage the exercise separately, following the scheme. They agreed, Steven wanted to start, and Marina remained on the sofa.

I invite Steven to choose somewhere in the room a *meta-position* and then from there to place three *spatial anchors* on the floor (round cardboards with position names), one for each *Perceptual Position*: *I*, *you* (the imagined partner), and an *observer*. The process involves four questions about the situation from the four mentioned positions, thus we obtain sixteen answers or statements for each person of which I kept notes. From there I was hoping to produce something tangible to hand over to both partners, lest I leave them empty-handed.

Soon it becomes clear that Steven is overwhelmed with the change of perspectives, the different questions, and simultaneously with the formulation of his thoughts and feelings; his answers often remain similar.

Important themes emerge, such as "his partner is always around", or "that one made the grade", and further that "he feels protected". I could not help but notice that Steven did not mention a word about his love for Marina or her happiness. The most important seems *to be loved by her*, a naturally present mother who provides safety.

I sense Steven's insecurity and his stress, and feel like I forced him into a task that is completely against his nature, he, who hates public presenting, who used to fear reading in school, who wants to appear cool—I forced him into a role, which exposed his helplessness in front of his partner, where he always wanted to put up a good show and to be at his best.

Have I betrayed him? I feel responsible for the little boy, who timidly confided in me with his misery, but I am lost myself, and cannot comprehend what is going on. Have I not made an unfeasible demand on him to manage his life, just like an older brother? From my own biography I know an internalised derogative brother's voice very well, too.

I feel terrible, unable to grasp or express my apprehension, just as young and helpless as Steven. Thus I simply continue blindly, utterly dissociated and stiff with tension, without any real contact with Steven or my mature-self. The questions become blurred for me as I continue.

We both act in a highly constricted state of consciousness, which contracts our mind, allowing little freedom of choice: the tunnel vision of the rejected, dependent, traumatised child. Steven in his dependent, insecure attached neediness is unable to switch perspectives. As for myself, I feel incapable of readjusting my self-state back into an open, calm wideness, out of which I stand a chance of holding and reliably accompanying Steven.

Throughout this process with Steven, Marina gazes out of the window and is apparently uninterested in her partner's efforts. My first thought is: neither is really interested in each other, they need each other! The thought frightens me, because they will definitely marry, and if I challenge the relationship would that not make me guilty? They should discover this by themselves, if it was true, I think. Perhaps I am wrong? Could she be averting her eyes in order to avoid him feeling exposed?

The chasm deepens

It is horrible; I have initiated something and suddenly I feel trapped. What now? I feel like everything goes totally wrong and that there is no contact at all, but I dare not stop the schematic procedure.

After over an hour, Steven has processed his four questions in four perceptual positions and I realise that the allocated time would be insufficient. Feeling hot and profusely perspiring, I ask whether they would stay an extra hour so that everything can take its space. Both agree, but nevertheless I feel extremely tight. Things seem to get out of control.

It is now Marina's turn to move through the *Perceptual Positions*. While asking her to place the spatial anchors, suddenly it appears to me as total nonsense, to place an imagined person on the floor, who is in fact bodily present. They could, after all, interview one another. "They have to look at each other!" I think, but do not know how to bring that into this awkward setting, in which I am stuck.

I become increasingly impatient, I wish the exercise was over, so that we might communicate again as living, feeling, human beings and I feel free and connected again. That state seems very far away now, like inaccessible ground.

Notwithstanding that, I grimly stay on course with Marina's exercise, forcing myself to calmness, lest I infect her with my mood, but instead give her some safety in the process. Finally I say to myself, that I do not bear responsibility for her emotions and it becomes a bit easier, recovering this lost boundary. I somehow manage to re-regulate myself.

Marina answers very clearly and manages the different positions well. She seems to be more empathetic and open. In her answers she mirrors genuine compassion for her partner, and she also wants to *give him love*. In me an image of mother and son briefly flashes up; she has a son more than a partner. And again the frightening irritation: is there any space for such a hypothesis? What would I trigger by mentioning it? Would it not imperil the whole relationship? Can I bear that responsibility? Is it not my duty as a therapist to take off the mask?

I feel in an embarrassing position and totally under pressure. After less than an hour she has proceeded through all questions. Repeatedly I notice for both partners, despite all difficulties, an unshakeable steadfastness of the common plan to marry. Perhaps there is a strong basic connection, on the other hand it restricts the freedom of developmental processes, if the result is already determined in advance and both partners anxiously cling to the once drafted plan, pulling it through at any cost, just like the procedure we are stubbornly following.

Should I point out this unshakeable steadfastness as a big resource for the shared coping of difficulties? I remember me mentioning this in the first session. I do not pick up this thread, but it feels like another wrong decision.

Narcissistic injury and parallel processes

Both partners sit next to each other. I feel hot, dirty, and like a miserable charlatan, as if I have wasted their time, and I expect their feedback to destroy me when I ask them: "What did you experience during this process?"

Steven concludes that it has been, and still is, very hard for him to speak about it, even to find words. He feels very agitated now and his thoughts seem more profound. I am surprised by that answer: could the process unexpectedly stimulate something out of my focus? I ask whether he has learned something new about his partner. Steven replies that he already understood everything before. He has nothing more to say.

Sadly confirmed in my bad estimation of the work, I ask Marina about her experience. She points out that she has seen Steven's capability to assume her position. "But emotionally I don't feel a single step further. I have only heard a couple of words."

Seemingly, nothing has moved. They have followed the exercise blindly without irritation, a parallel to their unshakeable life plan. It feels as an impossible task: change our problem, but do not touch ourselves. "Let me have my cake and eat it, too!" And me, too, I have followed the exercise unshakeably and thus have become their *complice* by avoiding to *focus on that very process*.

I confirm Marina's impression and apologise for the anaemic session and that the exercise might have been inappropriate here. Handing over the numerous papers with their answers and statements relieves me a bit like passing back the responsibility for the results of the process. But nonetheless everything feels empty and mechanical.

In order to add to this disastrous session a more lively, concrete, and bodily termination, I ask both partners whether they were in the mood for a little experiment. Thank goodness they become a bit curious again and agree.

I invite them to portray, one after the other, with both bodies a kind of sculpture: *the monument of our love*. Interestingly both monuments become mirrored: each one places the other partner behind himself, protectively hugged. As they see that, both giggle.

I marvel about that, do not know how to interpret this phenomenon: each one wants to be protected, no one wants to protect? I say: "You are in a way very alike. Probably you have found each other." Both laugh gladly.

I wonder how they have lived together without speaking to each other, and I see the courage it took to seek counselling. I feel a bit eased, that finally some simplicity, contact, and delight has entered the session, and try to find some closing words towards the obvious phenomenon that many things are better to see and comprehend beyond words.

Final words

Steven and Marina never came back together. There was only one last session with Steven alone, where he spoke of his great efforts in organising the upcoming wedding. His last news was an e-mail, where he explained that there would be no time for further sessions after being married. I do not know yet whether I should take that as a good sign. It is to be hoped that they have found their own way to real enjoyment with each other.

Triggered by the described experience, I try to give more trust in my intuition and my capability to spontaneously find or invent what is necessary in the moment. I share my own emotions, sensations, and impulses more transparently and courageously as a compassionate, equal co-actor. *Presence* is the term that bundles all qualities needed: simply being there with all we are and feel, as genuine living counterparts, not as experts. Being tangible touches and opens.

It is about immediate non-verbal communication and the embodied *being-in-the-world* (Merleau-Ponty, 1966) of all participants. I tried to create a glimpse of this with the finally added sculptural work, even though it did not transcend the enactment, which I unintentionally kept alive by my own collusion.

Phenomena like these arise from spontaneous *vegetative identification* (Reich, 1971), respectively *somatic resonance* (Keleman, 1990), the origin of all transferential dynamics, and the universal *mutuality* of the therapeutic relationship (Aron, 1997).

Every therapeutic encounter is an encounter with something fundamentally *unknown*. The transitional loss of orientation and control in countertransference is essential to our professional growth and maturity, often parallel to our patients. Thus they are also our teachers.

When all is said and done, all techniques are coagulated and structured former spontaneous interventions that should become replicable. Therefore we may permit ourselves to trust hands-on in emerging ideas. Techniques might be seen as friendly proposals of experienced colleagues. Today I *improvise* with exercises like the *Perceptual Positions*. So I can flow with the situation, remain present, using the tools instead of being constricted by them.

The aim is to stay in contact with myself and at the same time with the other(s) in a shared space: the *intersubjective third* (Ogden 1994b) or the *dialogic* phenomenal field of *being-with-the-other* (Merleau-Ponty, 1966, p. 389; Wenke, 2011, pp. 108 *et seq.*).

This open space seemed inaccessible to me in the displayed session, namely I had no memory that it existed. I took the mechanic exercise as my lifeboat. Carl Whitaker was known for saying that "techniques are things used while waiting for the therapist to show up" (Murray & Rotter, 2002, p. 204).

We all partook in collusive enactment of a procedural decision with little ability to reflect upon it or change it. Thus I acted in a defence *mode*, which occupied myself energetically and mentally, isolated my psychic field and inhibited a natural *resonant* encounter with both clients. Defence is less necessary if we stay connected with our mature safe, clear, and wide self-state or know how to regain it. We do this representative for our patients, too.

I was just as anxious as my clients: I did not dare to step out of the collusion. Was that only *responsive* countertransference or was I *reactive* (Racker, 1968), because of my former developmental state, simply incapable of going further than I did by the means I had at that time? I think the latter is true. Adler says aptly to his patients: "I can only heal you with the truth into which I have expanded myself" (Adler, 1928, p. 698). I met my own limits at that time.

For this painful reason I started working with a body-psychotherapist and detected my own trauma of abandonment and dismissal before my fifth year, where I was sent for six seemingly unending cruel weeks to a children's home far away. Back in my parents' home I remained mute for six months and froze in an oath for lifelong revenge. My confidence in love was poisoned for many years.

I have myself been a traumatised, abandoned, and lost child, which had prematurely fallen off the nest. After I had recognised and shared this experience, it is no longer an invisible but horrifying *phantom* in the shadow but instead *my own real agony* and coping reaction as a child in bitter hardships.

Continuous self-development, supervision, further training, and personal psychotherapy are all indispensable parts of our profession as counsellors or therapists. My daily meditation is an additional support to provide self-containment where I can reconnect with the wide shared space, beyond the defensive ego. Only he, who is wide himself can help others out of constriction.

CHAPTER SIX

Old ladies, exhausted souls, and a large sack of healing herbs*

Shinar Pinkas

Untouchable

D uring our first session, and in many that followed, she retracted from me. I used to look at her and she seemed to move uncomfortably; as if she could not swallow me. I wanted her to swallow me, to chew and take me in and secrete me and perhaps I would become of different matter. It did not happen. She did allow me to diffuse into her, and change her some; a tiny bit. I did something to her rigid structure, I reckon. I saw her softening over the years, allowing me to enter into her; very slowly. Entering her was painful, perhaps most painful of all. Each time she shared herself with me I would collapse. The thought that she exposed her fine capillaries for my sake was terrifying. "Don't do it!" I shouted from inside. I felt that she sold fine pieces of her own flesh in order to heal me. It must have been so difficult for her, I thought, and I needed it so. These were my significant stepping stones: when she let me into her life. This is when I understood how deeply I needed her; how I needed her to let me into herself. Allowing me into her guarded and protected world, opening this window, was also a metaphoric entry into her

*This chapter is dedicated to E. P and Y. M.

body; and all I wanted was to cuddle as a foetus within a nourishing body, her nourishing body.

She was neither my mother nor my friend. She was my psychotherapist and we both knew it from the start. Nevertheless, she had been to my wedding. I remember her telling me, "I cannot walk you down the aisle; but I can take these steps down with you," and this was the closest she had ever been to telling me "I love you". I have no doubt that she did love me, but also—and she attested to it on a few occasions—she could not fully touch me. Some places remained locked and sealed. Not only for her. I did not understand why she told me that I did not trust her, these words felt like psychobabble. I felt that I kept myself open, stretching the edges of my ability to be there, exposed. And it was not enough, like reaching a glass ceiling—something in me could not ascend. Something in me was missing, damaged, broken; I could not compete with her intellectual abilities. My heart did not open, I knew not how to love. My body wept; oh, how it wept. Mostly, the eyes remained dry.

I have learned from her about integrity. I arrived confused and chaotic, a black wing of a crow with a face of an autistic child; a faceless therapist, changing, and replacing names, colours, and personalities; nothing penetrated and all but passed through.

I wrote short stories for her: I do not know where they are today. I wrote about a million old women inside of me. I wrote about one hunchback woman, heavily treading the world with a sack full of healing herbs. She passed from one village to another, offering healing. When she finished, she moved to the next village. She knew no rest, this woman, had neither family nor love nor friends—only a sack full of herbs, which was forever full.

She loved my writing, perhaps more than she liked me being a psychotherapist. I desperately needed her confirmation. Initially, she could not provide me with her confirmation. She did not understand—and perhaps did not want to understand—body. She existed in her sharp mind and with her good eyes. Underneath this mind she had a body, but it was not a living, moving body.

The body as a subject of analytic enquiry

Meditation was a home for her; it allowed her a floating mindfulness that she dearly loved. She found it difficult to let go of this type of listening, and I wanted her to disconnect from it: I wanted her to tell me about sex, and love, and shame. I wanted to show her my inflated stomach, the one who did not know how to nourish itself with good food. I could not say it at the time but I knew all too well how to feel shame, and how to beat myself up with my compromised needs. I knew how to eat before sessions, so that my needy body would not be exposed; I knew not to expose myself. The food touched my body, rubbed against me. Before I saw her, I ate, and the food became an embrace.

We both relaxed in the sanctuary of the clinic; the world outside was harsh, angry, violent. Inside the room she really wanted me to feel good. I could not teach myself goodness. She taught me how to be on my own; how to bear this life. She taught me to be brave and honest, hardworking and real; to be honest with myself to the bone, to the flesh. Inside myself, it was who I was; she sculpted my inside out of me, a work of art.

She could not sculpt my body out though, she did not know how. She did ask me about bodywork, but these were not the right questions. I felt so ashamed, so I replied with omnipotent answers, and she was disgusted by these. I was disgusted with my body. Gradually, my body was erased. Bodywork treatments were erased too from my practice. My psyche strengthened as well as my intellect; I learned to think psychodynamically. I had a few good teachers, many bad ones; I've earned my diplomas.

The body became my drawing card: the thing that made me special, colourful—but also homeless, nomad, with a sack full of herbs on my back, and my body buried inside of it. People were interested in my body to heal themselves, but as soon as they finished using my body for their healing they no longer took interest in me. I never took the massage table out of the clinic but it became orphaned, and gathered dust. The number of clients who were invited on it decreased, the number of people sitting on the couch grew bigger. When I touched a body, I touched a loved body; this is what I felt. My client's body always responded. Even when it resisted or feared or angered, it was always touched—unlike the psyche.

But I abandoned the body. I started writing about the body, thinking it, conceptualising it. Not a bad thing after all. Once I asked her: what if there are untouched parts in therapy.

"Where aren't you touched?" she asked.

"In the body", I replied. There are certain parts that if left untouched—simply touched—in the body—they remain untouched. I did not say parts in my body, I could not. But she understood. She understood very well. And there was silence.

Once my supervisor asked me, seven years later perhaps, why did you stop touching?

I wanted to reply—I failed in my body. I could not be part of my body. I separated my body from me because it hurt less like this. I am therefore able to resist the desire to merge with any woman who could have been, in my eyes, a good mother. I now no longer feed the yearning to eat, to eat in order to thicken, to eat so I may stop hearing this body shouting, wanting to become; this body that emerged out of another body yet did not become nor took form nor received meaning, only endless words, meaningless buzz, words that teach nothing of the world.

Once in a while, my body threw a tantrum. I experienced it as a seizure of temporary insanity. I had become feverish, having to discharge anger. Discharging a whole harbour, an entire fleet of ships wishing to dock yet having no place, so time and again they crashed against one another. I did not know what to do with it besides getting angry and hateful, and hitting, and eating, and falling, and bruising myself and yet other bleeding body parts; and underneath the blood there was no friction, no touch, only an infinite pain laying curled up as a foetus wishing for someone to hold it.

Coffee and cigarettes

What did I need? This is the question waiting to be asked. What was it that I needed and had not received? And did I need it from her, within psychotherapy?

I left therapy after many years. It felt like mutual abandonment. Something was orphaned there, both concretely and symbolically. And when that something got orphaned it became emotionally easier to leave therapy. As for my body, it left therapy a long time beforehand: with great relief. And then my psyche was able to leave too.

My psychotherapist did well by me. In fact, I cannot imagine myself today without her. She is immersed in me, in the way I clinically work and think. But I did not learn how to move, I did not learn how to regulate myself. I did not learn how to inhabit my own body. I was only able to learn her and unable to learn beyond her; I did not realise *beyond her* even existed. I wanted her to remain my ideal image, the mother I always yearned for. She tried to deconstruct, yet she could not. I shut my eyes so tight, I was willing to dispose of my body, more and more, so I might feel like her. Rather, like how I perceived her to be, through my own eyes. I could not be a body because, in my experience, she was not a body. And if she was not a body, the only way for me to have her with me, to be with her, was to be bodiless.

She listened to me meditatively—gently, intelligently, sensitive to body sensations and breathing, a phenomenological stethoscope. I loved it most when she spoke in simple words, plainly. Her astute humour often liberated my distress. I did not want to be so frightened of getting closer; not to continuously check whether she was more accessible or resided in her meditative bubble.

I was so fearful of her not loving me, that each time she emerged out of her bubble I cried; perhaps I felt that I had to protect her there, from collapsing bodily. I feared that she would collapse from the demand I presented her with, to have a body. I could not express this, neither for me nor for her. Perhaps I had known that if I did ask, therapy would most likely terminate and I could not tolerate it.

She was bodily inaccessible. I was her client, and was not permitted in her body. It was closed before me, unexposed, private; too private, locked before me.

She did make me coffee. I remember how significant it had been for me. And she chain-smoked. Although I was not a smoker, I did smoke with her. Something of hers managed to enter me. Her coffee entered me and her cigarettes did too. It was not poison that entered my—it was real and different from the therapeutic yearning for emptiness, for emptying, to reach the threshold of consciousness.

Our shared body was a body of coffee and cigarettes—an addicted body, tired and dis-regulated; we were alike there too. We never spoke about it, did not attempt to transcend our own limitations, yet somehow—coffee and cigarettes have always been there for me. She made me coffee and handed me a cigarette and it was the most exposed we could be. She thus taught me how to keep company to the broken, dissociated parts of my body.

A short time before the termination of therapy she hung a picture above her. It was a painting of an old weary man with wise and exhausted eyes. His face was angular. I knew it was her who painted this face. There was so much of hers in this painting. She painted it when she was seventeen, she said, and decided to hang it now, hanging something of herself. Thinking about it now, she could not bring her body, so she hung it there.

The body in psychotherapy

I think that most therapeutic failures correlate to the degree of dissociation from our body. We are all both connected and separated from our bodyminds. Can we experience within life, within therapy, the degree of connection and separation? The places where our connection is faint, oscillating, prefers to not-be? Do I listen to the broken organs inside me? Are there body parts that are signifiers of arousal? Can we sense body parts where blood flows more? Where there is a stronger pulse?

How do I bring my body into therapy? Am I mindful of the ways my body is immersed in and with other bodies? Do I allow another body to enter me, to enmesh and immerse within me? And how do I do so? Which body do I bring into the room? How much does my body change? How much does it retract, present, is tired, falls in love, requesting, yearning, desiring to enter another body? How much does it recoil?

And how come psychoanalysis teaches us to lend our psyche and experience, our conscious and unconscious at the service of the client but we do not learn to lend our body? And what does it mean to lend our body at the service of the other?

I am looking at these questions and attempting to formulate these within my clinical work, to organise myself around them, to feel them. Frequently I am embarrassed: oftentimes I do not wish to lend my body. My mind is open, my body leans forward, yet it is irresponsive. When I cannot let a client into my body, when my body is not immersed in it, when I am unable to imitate the way he walks, his facial expressions; when I look at myself in the mirror after a session and something in my face has not changed or blurred—it means that therapy has not really worked that well.

When I do manage to leave my body into the other, I return differently. Sometimes I return with the other person's body and sometimes,

I come back alone. At times, I bring back gifts to my body; at others, I open myself widely for them to enter. It has a real danger. In any place where I am not in my body I experience penetrative invasion and sharp pain. Yet in each pore where my body and myself are one, I can expand.

Whenever the earth shakes under my feet, I need to be inside of me, to insist on being in my body so that the other would not abandon it. Winnicott remained in his body for Margaret Little. She managed to retract and return to her true-self because he was able and willing to lend her his body. He held her hands for long days so that he could be her womb; so that she may develop and blossom and grow and come out. He was first a mother and later an awake, sensual, sensitive body, which let her grow her own body and respond to it. And then a body that was ill. He was able to be all the bodies in the world; first and foremost he was an organism, a source of life. He gave birth to her and gave her a body. He taught her about body and change, and withering and withdrawal, about abandonment and hope and the capacity to be in her body and sense it wholly.

The containment Winnicott (1960; Little, 1977) speaks of is first and foremost a bodily containment—which body do you need me to be in order to grow? In this deep sense, it is not about which model or schema you need me to be, or what kind of therapist I can be for you—but a body. We are brought into this world by bodies, not consciousness. We learn about the world through our senses and experience it through our body. This is the basis for life. It should also be the basis for therapy.

Why is it so difficult to be there?

I have carried this question in my belly for a long time; for a very long time. The answer I can think of now, as I am writing these lines, is that it is difficult to be in our bodies all the time. It means that all the time, without pause, you are alive.

PART III

ENACTMENTS: WHEN BIOGRAPHIES AND SELF-STATES CONVERGE

Introduction to Part III

W e may argue that all therapeutic failures involve enactment, that psychotherapy and psychoanalysis are relationships, and relationships fail because of relational difficulties, where the self-states or the converging biographies of the parties involved do not allow for generative change, creating relational disso-ciation (Stern, 2010). Enactment happens when two parties matter to one another—and the more we care, the more we are exposed to hurt, and to hurting.

This section is dedicated to therapeutic engagements where there was a lot of care, or love, between the client and therapist. "Therapeutic action requires mutuality," wrote Lewis Aron and Karen Starr (2013). "We can expect our patients to reorganize their identities only if we are open to revising our own" (p. 43). What is arguably a necessary condition for successful relationship—mutual affective engagement—also makes us prone to convergences and enactments.

Three writers bring their highly personal account of their work. Sharon Ziv Beiman describes a meeting with "illegitimate" self-states, and the difficulty to own and acknowledge these. Shai Epstein weaves a personal story of parental neglect, terror, and shame with profes-sional enactment in attempting to save needy and wounded self-states of himself and his client. Last, Offer Maurer shares a fascinating case vignette of cycling around, and inevitably entering into the bullying and abusive cycles.

CHAPTER SEVEN

The fear of breakdown and the fear from 'breakthrough

Sharon Ziv Beiman

Nina (thirty-five) was named after her grandmother who, suffering from chronic major depression, committed suicide during Nina's mother's childhood. She had begun therapy fourteen years ago, due to symptoms of anxiety that included constant stress, a sense of being about to faint at any moment, extreme shyness, and a tendency to blush. These were compounded by a lack of belief in her ability to work, study, or handle her life.

When Nina was fourteen, her charismatic father had left her mother, informing Nina and her younger sister that for many years he had lived a double life with another woman, with whom he had another daughter. Nina and her sister took their mother's side. Nina missed her father's presence and admiration of her and was relieved when her relationship with him was restored years later. On the other hand, she described her mother as dependent, depressed, and introverted.

Nina described herself as anxious and avoidant in her childhood and adolescence, and experienced herself as academically and functionally incapable—also being aware, however, that others perceived her as beautiful and lovable.

The psychotherapeutic process very quickly generated significant improvements in Nina's self-experiencing. I empathised with her anxiety and fears. We co-narrated how her identification with her avoidant mother and suicidal grandmother led her to see herself as weak, helpless, and incapable, while her relationship with her father nurtured her belief that she was attractive, valuable, and capable. Based on relational psychoanalytic thought (Bromberg, 1998; Mitchell, 1993), I encouraged her to accept her multiple self-experiences—the avoidant, incapable, bright, and effective alike.

Nina felt empowered and vitalised by our relationship, sharing with me that in my presence she felt stronger and more capable, vital, and efficient. I believe that I had presented a new kind of meaningful other in her life—a warm and emotional woman who strives to act as an active agency in the world. Our interaction invited her wishes and abilities to interplay with me as a feminine version of her father. The intersubjective dyad was characterised by a natural collaboration between my dominant, pragmatic, functional-based, adoring, warm, and supportive self-states and her talented, dependent, smart, vibrant, ambitious, and charming self-states (Bromberg, 1998). The formulation of her emotions (Stern, 1983) and the interpretative contents were congruently assimilated into the intersubjective exchange between us, the matrix of our relational configuration converging with the therapeutic content to foster her personal development and growth, as well as significantly decrease her anxiety and distress.

Five years of weekly psychotherapeutic sessions empowered Nina and helped her to accept herself as an effective agent (Bandura, 1989, 2006; Pollock & Slavin, 1998; Slavin, 2012) capable of affecting others and achieving goals. During these five years, she gained a BA in Media and Communications, became an assistant in a well-known advertising firm, and entered a relationship with a young man who later became her husband.

One of the issues that remained unresolved during therapy was Nina's dream of becoming a writer. Although a short story she wrote during high-school years received high acclaim, she never followed it up with further writing, despite still dreaming of becoming a writer.

In addressing the disparity between her dream to become a writer and her avoidance of actually writing via a range of interventions, we focused first on understanding why she could not write, hoping that insight would help her to overcome the barrier.

Since the variety of interpretive narratives we had discussed did not enable overcoming the writing avoidance, I combined behavioural techniques within our psychodynamic therapeutic process, seeking to create cyclical change (in Wachtel's, 2014, terms) between behavioural, relational, and psychodynamic aspects of the psychotherapeutic endeavour. We tried writing workshops, personal guidance, scheduling techniques, and other avenues. I encouraged her to write without reflection—whatever came into her mind—in order to overcome her inner censors. However, none of our efforts had succeeded.

We then reflected on her need "not to write" and discussed whether the barrier stemmed from a fear of confronting self-states or emotional states against which she was unconsciously defending herself (Bromberg, 1998). We considered the possibility that her arrested drive to write represented an internalisation of her mother's and dead grandmother's unfulfilled dreams with which she unconsciously identified (Ogden, 1992)—and whether she was unconsciously afraid that if she wrote and published she might confront her guilt feelings towards her depressed and mentally-paralysed mother and dead grandmother (Modell, 1984). We also contemplated whether her unfulfilled dream of becoming a writer embodied her chronic narcissistic pain (Siegel, 1996)—the obstinate feeling of needing to write representing the successful person she hoped to become. Despite the knowledge that each of these interpretative explanations made good sense, Nina could neither overcome the writing barrier nor give up on the dream, and I did not cease from trying.

Following the end of our therapeutic process, Nina came several times for short consultations. When, for instance, she brought her fears that her son might be as anxious as she was, we easily and virtually directly returned to the psychotherapeutic channels we had created previously. The psychotherapeutic space was immediately and naturally restored and vitalised, helping her to experience herself as more powerful and to differentiate her fears from her weaknesses or her narcissistic pain from the way she had experienced her son or partner. At every session, however, she always came back to the pain of not being able to write, formulating this unresolved issue as the "real thing" we had to take care of one day.

In our final session—three months after the birth of her second son—she told me how much joy she gained from hugging her gorgeous children with her husband, the family unit forming a source of satisfaction and happiness. At the same time she shared with me her worries, her husband having been unemployed for more than a year. Although she understood how difficult this situation was for him, it made her feel a lot of anger at him for not finding another job so that she could resign from her senior position and fulfil her dream of becoming a writer. Speaking in a demanding and complaining tone characterised by a split from her joy around the enlargement of her family, she insisted I helped her in finding a way to free up her time immediately to write, nothing else was meaningful.

I suggested that we will reflect on the detachment I felt between her delight from her family on the one hand and the despair around not being able to fulfil herself on the other. Nina's response was immediate and stormy: "You don't understand me. Nothing will be meaningful if I don't start writing now. You have to help me make it happen . . . I don't want my life if I can't find a way to write now." She rejected all my suggestions to reflect on the gap between her need to write and the block around fulfilling it and any interpretative narratives I suggested.

I felt pressed and anxious by her demand for immediate change and the accompanied statement that she did not want her life unless we found a way for her to immediately write. My rescuer self-state was enacted immediately. In an authoritative manner, I asked that she pulled herself together and recognise that she was asking for things neither of us could provide under pressure. I asserted that despite my wish to be invested in working on enabling her to write in the future, right now I believed we needed to find a way to calm her distress and examine ways in which she could cope with her current life-demands.

The emotional atmosphere was highly charged. She felt I was attacking rather than supporting her and was weakening instead of strengthening her self-trust. I felt trapped in what I experienced as her fantasies about my magical powers, treating me as a fairy that could make her wishes come true. It was clear that we were experiencing a severe therapeutic rupture—characterised by a failure to find an authentic collaborative channel and therapeutic emotional exchange in a painful and overwhelming contradiction to our previous productive therapeutic interactions.

The session ended with me sharing my wish to find ways to open up dyadic supportive channels like those that proved helpful and empowering in our long therapeutic journey and to establish a sense of connectedness. She was not interested in arranging a further session, nor did she answer when I tried to contact her several days after our meeting. I have not spoken with her again since that point in time. I feel a lot of pain and distress around the severing of the long-term therapeutic alliance with Nina. During the next few years, I found myself obsessed over questions and thoughts regarding what had happened in that explosive session.

Understanding our "therapeutic crunch"—a defensive equilibrium, an intersubjective dyadic fixation, and mutual fear of breakdown

One of the causes for the dramatic impasse might be related to the negative influence of my working hypothesis that the unresolved avoidance she experienced around her wish to become a writer represented a defensive equilibrium (Searles, 1979). I assumed that while she experienced many positive changes in her life during the therapeutic process, this issue might represent unconscious conflicts or feelings with which she was as yet incapable of dealing since they served her psychodynamic defensive equilibrium. In Mitchell's (1993) words, I perceived her dream to write as a *wish* that represented an unresolved developmental conflict rather than a *need* that sought fulfilment.

Perhaps, had I conceptualised her frustration around her inability to fulfil her wish to write as a symptom that we failed to alleviate rather than as a defensive solution, I might have suggested trying additional therapeutic alternatives, or maybe I was retrying and deepening interventions we already had tried. Maybe then the severe therapeutic rupture would not have occurred and I could have addressed her distress and agony more efficiently, thus reducing her loneliness and frustration.

Reflectively, I strongly feel that the described therapeutic failure is linked to my virtually automatic reliance on the relational configuration that led to positive therapeutic changes during previous stages of the therapeutic process. I believe that when Nina came to our last meeting, she wished to share with me her joy from her enlarged family, together with a desperate need to contact dissociated and unformulated experiences, feelings, and identifications of herself—expressed through her cry for my assistance in finding a way to write immediately. I was enacted to formulate her complex mixture of feelings as a crisis that necessitated a crisis intervention, and addressed it with my functional oriented rescuer self-state. I could not open myself to look for alternative relational pathways through which to approach her pain and needs although I strongly felt that my reaction led to an interactional rupture. Although I was empathic at the beginning of the exchange, when she intensified what I experienced as demanding insistence, I rushed into my organising, rational, coherent, parental state. I may have been too eager to seek the comfort of our "base-camp" relational configuration, relying on its past efficacy rather than being open to the possibility that another position was necessary—willing to stay with her cry, validating her feeling that she had to touch and fulfil dissociated parts of herself in order to be able to continue to feel. When Nina insisted that she had to find a way to write now, I should have stayed with the pain and urgency and invited her more gently to explore her feelings rather than immediately structuring the situation with my interpretation of her needs, which was contextualised within the rescuer–survivor relational configuration. I was too heavily dependent upon previous spontaneous collaboration between my warm, assertive, functional-oriented, empowering, parenting self-states and her dependent, vital, efficient, charming, and lovable self-states that provided relief, enabled expansion of the ways she experienced herself and enrichment of her operational modes on the initial stages of the therapy.

Our therapeutic rupture can be thought of in Mitchell's (1993) words as "analytic crunch", a term Mitchell uses to describe "dark times in analysis"—moments of "impasse". In Mitchel's words, Nina and I felt during different previous phases of our psychotherapeutic endeavour that "we are working more or less comfortably together", meaning that Nina could use my interpretive understanding of her world via our relational exchange to "grow and expand her experiences" (p. 209). I believe that Mitchell would suggest that what enabled these productive therapeutic influences was Nina's success to suspend her dread that my interpretative perspective might challenge the mental equilibrium she had achieved through her life, an equilibrium that enabled her to partially fulfil herself but also constrained her mental existence. This suspension became possible since Nina perceived my interpretative work through the "prism" that had organised her subjective through her life—"The light that the analyst shines on the prism invariably enters it and is dispersed into familiar categories of experience: old dreads, old longings, old hopes" (p. 213). While the analytic productive comfort zones might characterise the therapeutic process for long periods, once the analytic understanding gets the potential to expand the patient's (and inevitably the analyst's) subjective "prism" they also inevitably threaten the mental equilibrium of the patient. These are the moments in the process where hope and dread are painfully evoked simultaneously, challenging one another. As Mitchell suggests some analytic endeavours never reach these dreadful–hopeful junctures and yet provide productive therapeutic work that does not challenge the patient's basic mental equilibrium. Some reach this dreadful–hopeful stalemate and succeed in redefining and transforming hope through a long and painful crisis, or through a few moderate crises. Unfortunately, I believe Nina and I failed to overcome the "hope and dread" impasse we encountered.

It may well be that the little child in me—forced too early in life to become a responsible mother to my own mother's floods of despair and distress—could not contain Nina's anguish, especially while bearing in mind that she was taking care of her infant son. It might be that my enacted reaction represented a *complementary countertransference identification* (Racker, 1957), meaning that I was mainly unconsciously identifying with Nina's baby, and hence trying to protect him and myself as a baby from meeting our mommy's despair. It might be that the danger I felt as a baby to contain the unbearable emotional pain of my mother and of myself prompted me to rush and pull her back to a balanced responsible self-state and to flee from what I had experienced in her as a dangerous emotional regression.

Perhaps, as a baby, Nina was also overwhelmed by the unbearable mental pain and suffering her mother felt, partially in relation to her grandmother's suicidal breakdown, which might have harmed her capacities to contain herself and Nina's intensive, chaotic, painful, rich, and colourful mental experiences, as well as constrained Nina's abilities to contain her own meaningful range of mental ingredients.

Maybe the convergence between mine and her "Fear of Breakdown" (Winnicott, 1980) had narrowed the transitional space, leading me to focus on reassurance, rationalisation, and organisation of her thoughts and experience, not allowing her to meet her need to regress in a holding environment and to contact her early dreadful and chaotic experiences as well as some dimensions of her vitality— experiences represented by the urgent need to "write" and that were dissociated as result of early traumatic breakdown in her bond with her mother that happened but was not experienced (Ogden, 2014).

What had created this urgent need to "write" herself and to contact painful, stormy, and maybe also libidinal and passionate aspects of herself? It might be that the interaction with her new baby, her second son, confronted her with dyadic experiences she could not bear. I believe that the birth of her second son intensified the gap between her conscious mental life characterised by striving to successfully adjust to life and other chaotic, painful, passionate, aggressive, annihilated, and empty experiences she had in relation to herself and to meaningful others in her life—which she had tried to dissociate. In Winnicott's (1980) terms, the gap between the *true-self* and *false-self*, or in Bromberg's (1998) terms the dissociation between self-states, had become unbearable. Her yearning that I will help her to "write" might represent the need to contact the dissociated aspects and to integrate them into her self-experience while confronting the dread that the meaningful dyads will not be able to hold the process for and with her, and will be destroyed (Ogden, 2014)—a dread that actualised itself in our last meeting.

I continue to analyse why our therapeutic relationship could not repair the dramatic rupture that captured me–us. Are my mental constraints responsible for this? Or maybe our souls unconsciously cooperated to defend her, me, and our dyad from what we unconsciously identified as dangerous experiences with destructive potential, including overwhelming positive and negative emotional qualities? Was the fear of breakdown in her subjective world and her meaningful relations with others, including her baby, displaced to our dyad, sacrificing it for the sake of avoiding breakdown? Or was it the limit of what I could offer as a therapist at that crucial moment that prevented the needed therapeutic action.

The therapeutic failure I described above took place five years ago. At that time I was not occupied at all with the wish to write and publish academic and professional papers. In the last three years, my own writing has become a major struggle in my life. I have many "half baked" papers and professional theses I would like to write, and I confront inner barriers that prevent me from actualising my need and wish to write and to present my own professional approach, experiences and ideas. I am occupied with my avoidance from writing and work hard to overcome the barrier with relatively partial success. I often think about the linkage between my therapeutic failure with Nina and my own struggle to write. Have we unconsciously and concordantly (Racker, 1957) identified with each other's fears of break-down that we might have experienced had we allowed the dreadful and creative dimensions of ourselves to invade our consciousness? Fears that resulted from early dyadic breakdowns that took place but were not experienced in our (respective) early lives (Ogden, 2014)? To what extent were my capacities to contain her needs at our last meeting constrained by an unconscious conflict I was not yet aware of?

The one thing I am confident about is that the process of writing about this therapeutic rupture serves my need to process the pain and concerns around what happened, and to discuss the harmful and defensive potential of the rupture concurrently. The inquiry into what happened, what was she crying for, and why I could not contain it, revealed the opportunity to better understand my own writing barriers while overcoming them through writing this paper. Although it will not help Nina, who I hope had found and will find channels to express her need to write, I would like to virtually share this enquiry with her to express the pain I feel for what we could not overcome together and for the sake of the continuous striving of all of us to fully experience and express ourselves.

CHAPTER EIGHT

Failing with dignity

Shai Epstein

S hould the therapy I offer be reduced to a dichotomy of success and failure? Could remaining in therapy be a failure sometimes? In writing about therapeutic failure, I risk narrowing the relational body psychotherapy I offer to a binary perspective. In my work I attempt to allow for a broader perception of reality, where we explore our shared meeting with curiosity and willingness to engage with our mutual involvement that a human encounter can bring with it (Aron, 1996; Epstein, 2013; Levy, 2013).

At the same time, I do not wish to avoid the meaning of failure for me. Failure can easily be wrapped in theoretical conceptualisation, distancing the possibility of engaging with real burning failure, turning it into a point of view, a possible interpretive analytic position.

Since I fail to objectively define therapeutic failure, I shall use this space to offer my own subjective experience: sensations, feelings, and thinking concerning failure.

Thinking of failures brings up a burning sensation in me, accompanied by bodily contraction and holding of breath. As a body psychotherapist, I attribute great importance to noticing my body in general, and breathing patterns in particular (Boadella, 2011; Gilbert, 1999; Keleman, 2012). Attending to these, I can recognise shame and self-belittling. I remember failures with a sense of burning, pain, and bleeding, but mostly shame and guilt. I recall grave losses, humiliating moments, being hit, disappointing my loved ones; times when I really wanted but the other did not . . . two particular events surface, one personal and another professional. I shall attempt to weave them together.

Oh, the shame

I just finished running down the stairs from home, on the third floor, counting the fifty-four stairs as I always did when climbing up or down. This time I was in a hurry, jumping down as I held the car keys in my hand, hurrying to my martial-art practice, worried that my sensei would be angry with me if I were late; but excited to leave the house. I sensed liberation and expansion in my chest as I stormed down the stairs to the ground floor. Suddenly, I notice four big people entering the building, the light is behind them so I can only see their contours: huge arms and massive chests. I slow down, sensing my expansion freezing with fear as one of them asks me bluntly, "Are you Shai Epstein?", waving an undercover police badge against my terrified eyes. I identify myself and they present me with a search warrant.

My breathing is arrested, my stomach contracted, I feel weak all over as I try to conceal their impact on me. An old, reliable mechanism is switched on, I dissociate; terror and fear are pushed down and I remain alert and minimally functioning, wearing a teenage façade of indifference.

Matters worsen; I do not make it to practice. Instead, three policemen search my room while the fourth sits with my shocked parents, frightening them with stories of juvenile delinquencies, drugs, institutions, ruined futures, court cases, and so forth. I sit there, absorbing the detectives' humiliation and mockery towards me and my parents' despairing looks. They have not conceived what came upon them at 19:00 on a Wednesday. I am silent, nearly immobile. I feel frozen and await the passing of danger, disconnected from feelings. Peter Levine (2005; Levine & Frederick, 1997) substantially writes about body freezing as a traumatic response, and certainly I am traumatised. An hour later they leave, having found nothing, leaving behind a court order to attend an interrogation the following morning. My room is in chaos.

Home is tense and silent. Then, my parents start speaking and I begin to cry. No longer can I hold back the tears of fear, pain, burden, and humiliation I managed to split thus far behind bars while the detectives were there. My sobbing does not feel liberating, it is heavy and shaming. I feel that I put my parents in a horrible position; I should not have allowed for that; I failed as their son, and am full of guilt and shame that keeps burning me throughout the night, a tormenting night full of obsessive thoughts about the suffering I inflicted on my parents and the failure that I have been. How could I humiliate them so? What did I do to deserve this?

A stormy beginning

I met Hannah for the first time in the evening, at the end of a long clinical day that started early in the morning. Once a week I come into the big city for an intensive clinical day, reaching the evening in different forms—sometimes void and lacking of empathy, at others in a dream-like state that helps me be clearer and sharper than usual, sometimes agitated and demanding. My defences are weaker, and I feel more vulnerable.

I feel ambivalent with myself during these hours. Over the years I noticed that I make more therapeutic mistakes in evening sessions, but I also challenge myself, the client, and our relationship more. It is a less defended and held time for me, carrying both promises and dangers, a fertile ground for therapeutic failures or extraordinary occurrences, moments of grace and transformation or acute empathic ruptures.

Hannah enters hesitantly, lean bodied, somewhat bony, and her face rounded with big green eyes, looking at me like a frightened gazelle. Her arms lay limp at the sides of her body. She sits with a regal flare and I feel delighted to have her with me in the room. Almost instantly I am full of empathy, curiosity, and a desire to know her. The levels of feelings and her impact on me frighten me, and I attempt to reorganise, regulating myself while concealing from her just how activated I feel. Hannah speaks of her reason to seek therapy and I hear her without listening to her words. She impacts me so forcefully; I am stunned by the feeling of falling in love with her, love at first sight. Shaken to my core, I struggle for my breath, holding an external façade of listening and coherency. Luckily, I have learned not to immediately show what I feel, to remain quiet and look attentive and wise; a priceless therapeutic technique. It buys me some time to digest Hannah's huge impact on me.

Holding this dual attention—inwardly and outwardly—is an acquired sublimation of my dissociative tendencies. Instead of splitting I hold both; trying to remember this while I turn my attention inwardly, in order to figure out what is happening to me. I notice that I do not feel sexually aroused but a deep, almost uncontrollable urge to envelope, hold, protect, and take care of Hannah. I can feel it in my hands, tingling with the wish to reach out. Some thoughts enter, interpreting the reality of my bodily experience, providing me with a rationale to hold on to, and I slightly calm down, my head now full of concepts, islands of understanding that allow me to rest, to a degree. Parental countertransference is easier for me than an erotic one, I think, feeling how I am gaining control and am slightly less lost and shamed by my desire to be near Hannah.

She looks at me; could she have noticed what happened to me? I wonder, perhaps she simply waits for me to say something.

Interrogation

I avoided my parents the following morning, waiting for them to leave for work, I did not know how to face them; and they avoided me too. I left home for the interrogation feeling small and lonely. Shame was so overwhelming that I was once again shut, unable to feel, frozen, and split, seemingly apathetic.

I await my turn at the police station. Policemen pass by; people are led handcuffed, screaming. Inside I am full of dread, while externally I feel rigid and opaque, trying to be cool . . . but miserably failing. The interrogator, who had seen many teenagers like me, breaks me instantly. He threatens and I break, shamefully beginning to cry. I have nothing of interest to tell him and he lets me go. I leave frightened, disappointed with myself, and with a burning feeling of failure—I failed to stay strong. Not only did I fail my parents, but I also disappointed myself now. I feel defeated, difficult feelings for a seventeen-year-old. I decide not to tell anybody about this experience; the shame is too big—it would be best to hide it. How can I tell anyone such a story? At home, life carries on as usual; we all avoid the subject. In my family, nobody asks personal questions, we are brought up to be independent from a young age.

Help the helper

"Suspend your subjectivity", I hear my supervisor's voice in my head and decide to keep my experiences to myself. I am as yet unclear about my experience with Hannah and therefore decide to maintain a somewhat distant, held-back position. During the next three sessions I mostly listen under the convenient guise of an intake, as Hannah unravels her life story. There is no father there, never was one, only a mother who struggled through difficult life circumstance and died a few years earlier. Distress and survival surround Hannah's life from every corner. She was born into and raised in this reality; at twenty-eight, lost in the world, she is looking for her way, time and again disappointed, but never gives up. The more she shares, the deeper I am swept into saving fantasies, heroic images of liberating her from her misery and finding the right path for her. Unlike the other people in her life who left Hannah on her own, it will be different this time! I will not abandon her; I can clearly see her distress, truly understand the preciousness of our unique opportunity together.

I refuse to recognise my enactment, fail to notice how arrogant my thinking becomes, how focused on a narcissistic saving fantasy—the power I imagine I possess to save poor, weak Hannah. This imagined power provides me with a sense of control over another part of me, which impatiently awaits our shared weekly hour; yearning for her to hesitantly enter my clinic, to sit, and spend time together. Something in our meeting fills a deep void inside of me, as I oscillate between a pre-oedipal infatuation with Hannah (Asheri, 2004; Messler Davies, 2003), a child in love with his mother wanting nothing except being with her, and the solid and strong paternal figure, who saves and promises never to abandon. And all this happens so quickly, I feel trapped between wanting to be saved by Hannah; to be held by her and enveloped by her, for her to never leave me on the one hand; and the soft, loving father that I am, wanting to take care of her, on the other. Both transferential images are vividly and concurrently alive in me, powerful, clashing against one another; I do not necessarily know who I am with her, but I seem to manage to conceal this turmoil thanks to the client–therapist role-play. Engrossed in my teenage self-state, I do not bring Hannah to supervision, not wanting to, feeling deeply ashamed. So, I remain completely on my own with her, noticing in a glance that my own patterns are perpetuated but unable to do anything about it.

Coming out

Years went by and I told nobody of what happened to me, wishing to forget all about it and move on. Seemingly, it worked; yet inside me I was preoccupied with these events, which fed my sense of failure and guilt: the burn. One evening, five years after the incidents, I was playing a game with friends—each had to tell a story about himself that nobody knew about.

As my turn comes, the story just pours out of me, like a loose cork; dread and relief envelop me. Shamed, I attempt to retrieve my dignity. My friends are all shocked, and one of them asks: "How come your parents did not help you? How come they weren't supporting you? Why did they not come with you to the interrogation?" (They went to work . . .) "How come they've chosen the police's side?"

I have no answers but these questions confuse me, disorientate me, change the way I constructed my narrative: it was my failure; it was my responsibility and my fault! The possibility that my parents were not there for me did not even cross my mind, the thought that they could have been supportive of me, accompanying me to the interrogation, paying for a lawyer—taking care of me when I faced big and scary forces did not occur to me at all; a foreign and unthinkable possibility. Realising I was abandoned, having to deal on my own with a situation far too complex for my age, I begin to laugh. My friends look at me, worried, not understanding what is happening, but I laugh and laugh, without realising it letting go of an old burden. The burning in my chest is slightly eased and the sense of failure and guilt softens.

In later years I process these events in different ways. I can see this repeated theme of being abandoned when in distress, as authority figures are unable to contain me when I am weak and in need of protection. I too struggle to contain my weakened self, and abandon myself as well. A deep sense of failure, coupled with shame and guilt, is tattooed inside of me. This insight helps and gradually eases the burden from my chest, and I learn to claim my need for (and right to) being taken care of and cared for without feeling ashamed.

The inevitable fiasco

Hannah finds it difficult to expose herself and speak of her life; it involves pain and almost necromancy—bringing unformulated and untouched memories to life, but she bravely faces this challenge. A month goes by; Hannah feels safer with me, her posture seems more relaxed; her gaze less frightened and suspicious, and she shares more of her life with me, showing me what nobody has seen before. It seems that Hannah is detoxing, mobilising areas that were at an impasse for many eons, reintroducing pulsation (which is understood, in body psychotherapy, as indicative of health (Boyesen, 1980; Keleman, 1981)). It looks as though I am doing my job, allowing her space and containment; yet inside I continuously move between wanting to save her and wishing to fall asleep in Hannah's arms. It becomes increasingly difficult, I am ashamed of needing her, ashamed of sensing my neediness, and of its very existence within the therapeutic relationship, but I cannot stop myself from feeling it.

Towards the end of a session I suggest we extend our session times, I feel bad for finishing on time; it is as if I abandon her each and every time. I can almost see her pain every time the hour comes to a close, and I suggest an hour-and-a-half session.

Hannah is taken by surprise: "Why are you suggesting this?" she wonders, "I cannot afford paying more." I fail to hear the tension in her voice, the warning. Preoccupied with myself (but certain she is on my mind), I declare: "you won't have to pay more money; it is important for our process." Hannah stares at me, I feel that I have missed something but cannot tell what it is. The atmosphere changes and I sense Hannah's withdrawal. "What's happening in you as you hear my offer?" I ask. Hannah is silent. Making no eye contact, she reiterates "I don't get why you are suggesting this, I am supposed to feel happy or grateful but I don't. I feel ashamed by your offer, as if you offer me charity. You seem to want it more than I do," she says.

I do not know how to respond, I feel exposed, caught, and frightened. Hannah has felt what I thought I managed to hide all this time:

"You are right. It is my wish to extend our sessions; I find it difficult to end them after an hour. Think about it and we can talk about it next week," I say, and feel avoidant. I failed.

Hannah leaves the room and I remain with a harsh sense of heaviness and wrongdoing.

I have not seen Hannah since. She called a few days following that session, saying she would rather not come to therapy anymore, that I confused her and she was unclear about what I offered or what I wanted from her.

Summary

The teenage memory I shared here expresses an essential part of what made me into a therapist, the wound I came from (Winnicott, 1963), of dissociating myself from my own emotional needs in a relationship, being attentive to the other and less to myself. This required a long and tedious training (Miller, 1981)—being the listener, the one who is ok, against whom you can lean. This is the habitual position I developed as an abandoned child who should conceal his weakness or failure; the one who bears great loneliness and confusion about being open in an intimate relationship. But meeting with Hannah penetrated this sheath; she shook me. Her presence powerfully awoke in me, with unfamiliar force, my own needs inside a relationship. I certainly failed to resolve the mutual enactment and collusion with Hannah, but today I feel neither shame nor guilt about it. Our meeting was a cornerstone in my initiation and personal growth journey. It took me many years to process what happened to me with her, the sense of failure, guilt, and shame for what I felt and how I acted; but the processing changed me. My needs in life and with clients became clearer and more accessible for me, and managed to appear clearer and more lucidly in therapy. As I allow these an appropriate space inside of me, I also negotiate what to do with these needs in therapeutic sessions.

I am still fighting for my right to fail with dignity; to disappoint another, to avoid succeeding at all costs without feeling shamed about it.

CHAPTER NINE

A Failure with a capital F

Offer Maurer

M any years ago, my supervisor at the time made a comment that has stayed with me ever since. "I mess up quite a lot", he said to me. "Actually, I say nonsensical things pretty much on a daily basis . . .". We laughed together. His comment followed my report of a questionable intervention of mine, so his response was spot on. Still, it was quite surprising to me, both because I had come to idealise my supervisor quite a bit at the time, but also because other supervisors never made a habit of sharing their failures (or even the fact that they have ever had any). Over time, I came to learn that doing therapy means being in a world that is fraught with inaccurate turns, repeated impingements, and unfortunate failures. But what does constitute a failure in therapy? For me, some failures in therapy seem to feel subjectively different from others. What is it that makes some failures stand out to become personally-experienced as Failures with a capital F? This chapter will focus on certain internal processes in the therapist that seem to be implicated in such Failure dynamics. What is a Failure with a capital F, and how is it different from the more "common" ones?

Using emotion as a compass to these somewhat dangerous territories, I would like to propose that a Failure is a failure that hurts a great deal. It resonates and touches deeply, and stays there like an open wound that will not easily heal. The fact that it hurts so much (and in a very particular manner), actually tells the story of the deep place from which the original problem-dynamic has evolved in the first place. Whereas daily failures happen due to many different reasons, I have come to learn that the story of therapeutic Failures is a story of painful relational re-enactments. Whereas failures (with a small f) could be the result of lack of knowledge or skill, I propose that Failures with a capital F are many times the result of an intersubjective clash that has to do with past experiences of both parties involved (Bromberg, 1991, 1996; D. B. Stern, 2004).

Though contents of Failures vary considerably, the underlying dynamic, I suspect, is often the same. An old scenario gets triggered for the therapist within the relational matrix, but due to various reasons (to which I will soon return) he or she fails to see this. In stark opposition to other instances, in which the therapist's old dynamics and participation could have been observed, metabolised, and recognised in a growth-promoting manner, in Failure dynamics, the therapist misses out on the repetition aspect of what is going on, and thus is unwittingly pulled into a major re-enactment of some old script from his or her own past (Bohleber et al., 2013).

Actually, one could say that to a certain degree, this is *always* the case and in *every* therapy. Every therapy, arguably every human encounter, has the potential of evoking long-standing defensive, hurting, hurtful, or other kinds of self-states in us (Bromberg, 2011). But in Failure dynamics, I propose, therapists utterly fail to grasp their own participation. Everyday little-f failures are those re-enactments or entanglements that can serve as stepping-stones for change and growth, ones that give us a chance to repair ruptures or to emerge jointly out of some impasse. In contrast, in big-F Failures, we simply repeat the past in some very familiar and constricted manner. Thus, Failures with a capital F occur whenever we are blind to our own participation; these Failures are ever so painful precisely *because* we are often so profoundly blind exactly where it so terribly hurts.

A case

When I first saw Joe he was extremely depressed. In fact, I remember thinking to myself that he must be one of the most tormented people

I have seen in my whole life. Joe was thirty-seven, fair skinned, green eyed, and very good looking, but when discussing his self-perception he described himself as nothing much to look at. He contacted me after seeing a couple of therapists with whom he had not connected well: "I never liked those silent, nodding type therapists," he said. He told me he had been depressed ever since he could remember himself, but that the depression worsened after losing his mother to cancer three years ago. She died in his arms at home while waiting for the ambulance to arrive, and he never quite ceased mourning her loss ever since. Various anti-depressants did not help. In our first session he told me he wanted me to help him to "get a life, and soon", but after telling me he was gay and "deep in the closet", he quickly added he will "never come out, so no use going that way with me, ok?"

As I got to know Joe better, I suggested we adopt an integrative approach (using the Schema Therapy model) to which he gladly acceded (Young et al., 2003). His cautionary tale (Ogden, 1989) about the silent nodding therapists made me surmise that he may be asking for a different kind of parenting in therapy than the flaccid, non-involved one he got at home as a child. We started off working towards the creation of a "case conceptualisation" that was to guide our work together, and Joe became quite taken by the process.

As therapy progressed, Joe told me about the severe emotional abuse he suffered as a child. He had been continuously bullied by his two older sisters and by other kids at school, and neither his parents nor his teachers defended him. In fact, his father seemed to him to be enjoying the abuse quite a bit, perhaps secretly hoping it would toughen Joe up. His mother was simply absent. His sisters would call him a faggot, physically abuse him, and go out of their way to find cruel and hurtful pranks to humiliate him in front of others. At the same time, and with no sense of internal coherence, he felt his entire family to be admiring of his high intelligence and that it was his destiny to save them from poverty and its accompanying shame.

The years in junior high school were rough. Joe became acutely aware of the fact that he felt attracted to other boys, a shattering realisation—his worst nightmare coming true. He saw this as a proof of the veracity of his sisters' degrading attacks, felt ashamed and defective, and was sure he would never be able to fulfil his life's mission of saving his family. His life-long pattern of withdrawing from society into fantasised daydreams of great riches and success became increasingly pronounced. His mother did try once to ask him what was going on, but when he waved her off she seemed to lose interest and did not address him again on the matter. He remained silent and distant, very depressed and barely involved socially ever since.

An important part of therapeutic work in the Schema Therapy model involves identifying the main self-states ("modes" in the model's terms) that are implicated in the patient's suffering (Rafaeli et al., 2015). After doing so, the therapeutic dyad ideally works together in order to activate those major self-states and engage them in the session, so as to enable the meeting of previously unmet core emotional needs. In the conceptualisation we co-created, several of Joe's self-states were identified. One of these was that of a lonely child—a sad and vulnerable kid, whose only solace was in his books and in his walks in the woods. An additional, other–pleasing and obedient self-state emerged as well, one whose main function was to make sure nobody would ever hurt little Joe again. Another very prominent self-state that emerged was that of an extremely hurtful internal critic who ceaselessly (self-)bashed Joe with harsh words, impossible demands, and sometimes even vulgarities, calling him a "disgusting faggot" and more.

As therapy progressed, our goal became clearer: as suggested by the Schema Therapy model, we needed to activate the vulnerable child self-state in order to meet some of its unmet core emotional needs (i.e., safety from abuse, respect for who he truly is, etc.) (Rafaeli et al., 2011). In other parts of the work, we also needed to activate the internal critic so that it could be transformed through some direct confrontation by the therapist. All of this was to be pursued using experiential chair-work and memory-rescripting in imagery work.

Initially, the plan worked quite well. Joe was moved to tears in a number of sessions as we got in touch with his sad and lonely child self-state. This plan often used imagery work as well as chair work, in which I provided him with the sort of protection against his ever so malicious internal self-critic (identified as the internalised voices of his sisters and father). In all of this work, I took the side of the "healthy adult", defending little Joe against his abusers, powerfully confronting them, and providing him with support and validation, both in sessions and sometimes between them, over the phone, at difficult times of crisis (Behary, 2013). "Little Joe" seemed happy and relieved to get my protection, yet he also seemed a bit anxious, as if something was wrong. Trying to enquire about this led to a dead end.

About a year into therapy Joe met a gay man at the gym and decided to pursue the relationship. Pretty soon, it became clear that the guy was adamantly against Joe being in therapy. "Either it's because he was hurt by therapy before, because he has some issues with god and psychotherapy, or because he saw too much crap on TV", Joe explained the opposition, and added, looking quite ashamed to say it, that "we will need to keep our appointments secret so that I could keep seeing this guy". A secret? What is going on? I thought to myself and proceeded to enquire some more. But soon, the partner made it very clear: either Joe chooses being in therapy (a relationship with me) or being in a relationship with him. "It's an either-or situation", he explained to Joe. "Plain and simple, just like that."

As you can imagine, I was troubled by (but also intrigued with) the forcefulness of the partner's demand, and even more so, with what I saw as Joe's faint, submissive reaction. He seemed to almost enjoy the situation. I invited Joe to look at the possible meanings of what had been going on, and especially at his own internal reactions, but he responded with very little interest, and finally told me he was choosing to go with his partner and discontinue therapy. This choice truly surprised me. Looking back, I think that at that point in time some part of me still did not really believe he would actually terminate. "Maybe you feel you need to go out there and fend for yourself, take what you've got in therapy and put it to work out there, in the real world, without me by your side?" I surmised. Associations started to flow. He said that for a while now he felt angry with me for needing to pay for therapy and also angry for the fact that he started to feel like he truly needed me. I was so happy he was able to feel (let alone express) all this assertive anger. I raised the option of keeping up the work together, with me being more aware of the change that had transpired in him, more aware that he has grown and matured. That now we can *both* see Joe not only as a the vulnerable lonely child but also as a grown-up man, a "healthy adult" in his own right, and that we could see me not only as a surrogate parent, but also as his equal in many ways. Tears rolling down his cheeks, Joe said "Thank you". A long silence ensued. "But I will stop coming here. That's my decision." It sounded so conclusive, I felt that I just could not say a thing more.

So much was going on inside of me at those moments. Should I support this step? Should I not? Despite my misgivings, I think now that my belief that Joe's autonomy (as shaky and brittle as it was) was of utmost importance at that moment, ultimately shaped my decision. But first I disclosed all of my reservations, the reasons for my being so torn. Joe listened attentively, expressed his understanding, and voiced a sense of happiness given my bottom-line decision (i.e., that I would support his will). I invited him to return if he finds the need, and he thanked me for this invitation. We continued for a few sessions more, summarising together what had been gained in therapy and what had not. During those weeks, my work with Joe felt like some kind of a failure—though not a capital-F Failure. I felt sorry that he terminated too soon (for me?). I felt some guilt, maybe even some shame. But looking back I remember telling myself he *will* be coming back. I was in a self-soothing self-state, no doubt. Some deeper pain must have been there.

Nothing prepared me for what was to unfold. Three months after termination I received a text message from Joe, saying:

> Thank you very much for the lesson I learned from you, the one which is really the best one for life: If there's no money in the horizon, then there's no caring nor interest. Oh, and by the way—I AM a disgusting faggot and that's how I'll forever be: a sick fuck that's not good for anything. Best to you and good luck with everything. Thank you. Please NEVER contact me again.

I was shocked. Getting this message felt like a kick to the stomach. Oh my god, I murmured, where did that come from? I read the message over and over again, not believing my eyes, trying to salvage some hidden meaning that must be encrypted in there.

Maybe I should not have "let" him go . . . Or maybe one part of him did need to feel me letting go of his hand, but then a different part of him expected me to reach out to him after termination, to check how he is doing. He seemed to have been waiting for me to woo him into therapy again, invite him back. Was I tested and failed the test, and miserably so? Was I just like all the rest, who used, abused, and deserted him? I felt that the part of him that was testing me, and that wanted me to lose, won this one out. A bitter victory for that part of him, a bitter loss for other parts—and for me. A zero sum game. It hurt so much. It still does. To me, this feels like a Failure with a capital F.

Another difficult dynamic that got spelled out in Joe's message was the victory of the internal critics and abusers. This, of course, is closely connected to the test I failed (by letting him go), a proof those parts worked so hard to obtain, and finally did. They won the war over Joe: "they" were right. The other parts (the attachment-seeking and self-soothing parts) and me, we all were in the wrong. Looking back at what had transpired between Joe and me led me to re-think the practice of directly and forcefully taking on the internal malevolent self-states of my patients. I already had some doubts about this practice beforehand, but this turning of events really got me to reconsider my practice in these dangerous terrains.

A short while after these very painful events with Joe, I attended an intensive workshop with Suzette Boon, the internationally renowned trauma expert whose best known for her work with patients suffering from dissociative identity disorder. I guess my attendance in this workshop was not chance, as something within me was still looking for some answers. After watching the session tapes she presented I was struck by the tremendous amount of respect and gentleness she showed towards some pretty horrific malevolent self-states (i.e., parts) within her patients. This stood in stark opposition to the very confrontational approach sanctioned by the orthodox Schema Therapy model, which has quite a lot of rigorous research evidence to support its claims (Arntz et al., 2005; Bamelis et al., 2012). I came up to her during the break and asked her about this discrepancy. Her answer was both telling and timely. Boon told me she had also received training in Schema Therapy and had attempted confronting those malicious self-states in the manner prescribed by the model. The results, she said, were problematic. Whereas in-session, the patients seemed to be experiencing some relief, at home, those internal-attackers came back with even more vengeance. Some patients, she said, would then need even more care and protection due to an increase in their suicidality. These experiences led her to change the way she worked with critical or punitive self-states to a way that is much more respectful and gentle (S. Boon, personal communication, May 18, 2011).

Why did I not see this before? All the signs were there. Joe was doing better in the sessions but not making any improvement outside of them. Throughout our work he seemed as depressed as ever. Maybe what happened was that I protected him in the sessions but then, at home, he again got bashed by those internal attackers. I thought about the reasons for my blindness to this dynamic. At first I thought to myself that I was just following the clinical prescriptions my teachers had taught me. But this did not seem to be the whole story. It is rare for me to dutifully comply with clinical dicta without thinking them through to see if they fit my clinical understanding and personal style. What was it then? I came to remember those highly-charged sessions in which I so bravely stood up against Joe's abusers and attackers. And suddenly it hit me. As I was fighting hard to save little Joe, I guess I was *also* fighting my own battle. I was fighting so save myself, or my young self, who was also powerless, very confused, and all alone in the face of other children's mocking, hurtful attacks. I still hurt inside as I am writing these lines. I guess I could not empathise with Joe's abusers as long as I could not find any understanding for my own internal tormentors.

The hard lesson I learned with Joe changed the way I now work with malevolent self-states, opening up new possibilities for me to free myself from the grip of the past. Today, when I encounter such self-states with my patients, I often view them as internal representations of parents (and others) who just did not—and maybe still *do* not—know how to treat their children right, mainly because of their own deficient upbringing. After realising I am not against them, these self-states usually coyly come out to seek counsel with me. Most malevolent self-states I have encountered to date really did not know any better. They taught me they crave closeness and understanding for themselves. They have shown me that it is often really hard being so rough . . . . Many of them agree to change their ways after getting enough reassurance and guidance from me. This adjustment I made in applying the Schema Therapy model has helped me personally to make peace with some of my own self-states. I got quite a bit from my Failure.

PART IV

AFFECTS ON THE EDGE

Introduction to Part IV

Stephen Mitchell (2005) emphasised that if the patient does not get "under the analyst's skin" (pp. 5–6), then the therapeutic process is limited in scope. Relational psychoanalysis, in its emphasis on mutuality and affect, also brings us closer to the edge of rupture, since both parties are involved, vibrating and vital. Perhaps the potentiating therapeutic position is also at risk of fragmenting and dissociating, that although we need ruptures for repairs and reorganisations to take place, not all affects are survivable by the client, the therapist, and the therapeutic dyad.

There are certain times when some affects are just impossible to bear. Homeless, these affects spill into real life, or into the margins of psychotherapy: beginnings and endings, e-mails and text messages, words spoken at the doorknob or words never spoken at all. These affects may include the murderous, the envious, the raging, but at times also the erotic, the needing.

Two analysts contributed to this section of dealing with strong affects, affects on the edge, which at the time are too volcanic to experience, Muriel Dimen and Asaf Rolef Ben-Shahar speak of affects that are too frightening to bear, where the tension between the symbolic and real, the analytic and the involved seem to collapse. Barbara Pizer painfully looks at times when rage and anger remain unexpressed and only partially-experienced, thus limiting the capacity to create intimacy and fully engage with one another.

CHAPTER TEN

Like a drop at the lip of a glass

Muriel Dimen and Asaf Rolef Ben-Shahar

Muriel: Hold on, someone's at my door. I can't imagine who it is. [*speaks into intercom*] Hi, I think we're on for noon. You want to come into the building? Can you come back? I also have time later this afternoon, but I suspect it's not good for you. . . .

Asaf: This was very dramatic.

M: This day is bad. That was a rescheduling, and she often gets it wrong. Talk about failure . . .

A: Perhaps we can begin with you sharing how has the subjective experience of failure changed over the scope of your practice?

M: Well, I'm thinking about the kinds of failures are there. How do you know when something is a failure? You only know it afterwards. There are ordinary failures, like today in the three sessions preceding this conversation, and what I would have felt about them when I first started, and what I feel now, well into my practice. Back then, when I felt there was a failure—I had wounded somebody or there was a failure of connection—I would be very alarmed, I can feel it now. And that alarm would carry through to the next session. Then I would be surprised and relieved to see that there was still a relationship there.

A: That the attachment lasted.

M: Yes. Consider this: I have just acted out at the end of the last session. I know it's an enactment, but I am very distressed by it, and there is a touch of an alarm—but I also know by now that the attachment endures. I don't expect it to be a therapeutic failure. It's a treatment that has gone on for many years. But I am disturbed and it takes thinking. Perhaps that thinking should never go away; I am in the middle of it, and in the middle of it you feel alarmed. Levenson (1983, p. 69) says that when analyst and patient are both disturbed that the analysis begins.

A: So how do you process this alarm?

M: Personally—I now have to wait until I see her on Friday. And then I have to see whether she actually remembers what happened at the end of the session because sometimes she doesn't. Or, better, sometimes she remembers what I remember, and sometimes she remembers something else that is more important to her and/or more pertinent to where we are.

A: So you are waiting to process it within the relationship.

M: Sometimes you actually can do it alone. Sometimes, when I have my own space, I can process it in such a way that not only does the mistake make sense in terms of the immediate context, but also there are other contexts that can arise and then something that I was never able to make sense of before makes sense, and then my disturbance decreases. At other times it may not be possible to resolve it alone. I guess we talk about the feeling of resolution, until the next time you meet with the person.

A: And are there failures which are impossible to process? Not just with the patient, but also inside of you?

M: Yes. For example, when somebody left treatment, they did not terminate but went back to using drugs. The fee was very low. So was it that they *wouldn't* afford it? The person was now married to their self-medication. And there was no understanding, as a result of mistaken interpretations and disclosures on my part. I didn't hold the symbolic place with that patient. So what was happening collapsed too much into the real, into the material real in the process of disclosure. I would not make that mistake now.

One of the elements of psychoanalytic work and any kind of serious work is learning from your errors. I have learned that there's a
certain state of mind that needs to be maintained and I can be increasingly sensitive to it, and when I feel that state of mind collapsing, I
know that's a sign to check myself and check what I am saying and
what I'm about to say. That state of mind is a suspension between
action and deadness, like the surface tension of a drop of water at the
edge of a glass, how it hangs there. That's the state of mind I think one
needs to be in.

A: How is this surface tension different from a transitional space?

M: There's a tension, one feels it, and it's a feeling of simultaneous
involvement and watchfulness. Winnicott described transitional space
from the outside. I am evoking a tension as it is experienced. It may
be that it characterises the state of mind one sustains in transitional
space. Or in participant observation. In any event, that tension
collapsed just now with this patient at the end, by the doorknob. For
her, it's about the end of sessions, which is very painful for her but the
absolute pain of it we've only been able to put into language now, and
it has to do with the number of minutes in the session, and how I
would never go over, how I am always cheating her over time, and
how I have my eye on the clock.

I know when a person arrives because they buzz my outside door.
One time I was five minutes late and she was three minutes late. So I
let the session go over its regular end by two minutes, and she was
furious about it then and brings it up from time to time. It happened
years ago. Is it about something else? I think so. But she deems me
picayune.

Recently, I told her—and I am not sorry about this disclosure—that
I feel guilty every time, at the beginnings and ends of sessions. I still
need to tell her that I'm tired of being blackmailed. Today, at the end
of the session, she said, "I was just looking at the time and I see you
started a few minutes late, maybe because I was a minute late and you
went over time with the person before me, who was just leaving
before I came in." And then I said, and that was my mistake, "You
don't know what she was doing, you don't know when she left . . . she
might have gone to the bathroom." She said, with a triumphant smile,
"She never goes to the bathroom after her session." Anger filled the
crack in the door between us.

A: The landlady of time (Dimen, 1994), and here enters power
dynamics.

M: One of the things about power dynamics is the affect that accompanies them—the anger, aggression, rage, the submissiveness, and so on. A question comes up, though, about the interpretation of affect. When I have interpreted rage to this patient, she often objects. If she is conscious of rage, we can discuss it as such. But if she is not, my interpretations are unacceptable because they feel totally off-base to her. So in my moment of enactment, I feel that I was holding her rage: at least, that's what I read in her triumphant smile. But I had provoked the manifestation of rage by being defensive.

A: Isn't making you feel guilty one of the ways for compensating for the humiliation, the a-priori bias of power dynamics? You are made to feel guilty, you are furious with the guilt . . . it's a way for her gaining an upper hand.

M: Yes, in fact, my attempt to gain the upper hand by being defensive actually backfired. But I'm also humiliated because I can't be a good person in this moment—I'm holding anger, and I did something really stupid and infuriating at the doorknob. Power dynamics come with great affect, and I wonder if this is one of the reasons that it can be hard for people to negotiate—because the affect is so strong. When we're in the realm of power dynamics we are talking about murderous feelings. I believe it would help her if she could experience the aggression with me, but that's probably met by my own anxiety, there's probably a mutuality—and mutual fear of the inability to regulate.

A: So you trust your own rage as a self-object more than you trust hers. Holding it on her behalf, it's easier to trust your own regulation.

M: Possibly. She was certainly the subject/object of uncontrolled rage in her life.

A: And the strong affect holds the potential for resolution but also for shame and guilt and enactments that might fail.

M: I think that shame and guilt come up when rage and fury can't be experienced in their pure form—then there has to be hiding, projection, and projective identification, and then shame and guilt bloom. Doing it at the doorknob is a chickening out. But that's how it tends to happen. To be able to have the anger in the presence of the other and express it with force—I think, depending on what's said, that could be cathartic and allow the experience of genuine engagement.

A: And when rage is left in the ether, in an unregulated space, it leaves both parties distressed.

M: It festers, it gets infected. True, I'm apprehensive of getting the affect, but I think I should receive the expression, but now it festers in her and then she may dissociate it. Or she may remember it but be disconnected from it.

A: When I was in the army we were told that military training is the opposite of being human—when you're shot at, instead of running away from the fire you run towards it. In a way, you are saying something similar.

M: Yes, and the running towards took place in a cowardly way. It was my responsibility. Steve Mitchell (2000) said that at the heat of the session the analyst is the designated driver.

A: Are you attempting to role model the courage to engage?

M: I suppose so, though it was not part of my conscious conduct of myself that I'm role modelling, but in effect it is. You know, as a patient I never thought about my analyst as being dependent on me for their income. I thought they had all the money in the world (that is to say, they have anything they need). Recently, it was clear that my analyst was wanting something from me. But this wish was immediately discussable.

A: Does discussability safeguard against relational failure?

M: There's going to be failure. We may wish for sameness and we may wish for difference but there is a very fine line when the desirable difference becomes too much difference—becomes inimical. So there's always going to be relational failure, there has to be. Otherness means that we're going to get each other wrong.

This is where failure becomes a sliding signifier—there's the treatment that just ended badly, and there's the treatment where there were a series of ruptures and lots of repair work. Rupture and repair become an inevitable part of therapy: failure, rupture, and repair. We do that over and over again. The ideas of enactments, of rupture, and repair, are spread and part of the paradigm shift today.

Failures can be ongoing—a real blind spot that your patient keeps pointing it out; and there could be a mutual acceptance of your inevitable failure in that. And then there are "ordinary" failures, some with a great deal of affect like this one at the doorknob, others with less. If you're going to learn something there has to be something you don't know; and if you don't know then that can be distressing sometimes.

And there is, of course, the failure of the relationship. I got an e-mail yesterday from someone who is thirty-two. I started seeing her when she was seventeen, and saw her off and on for nine years. When she was at college we did phone sessions. In the spring she was back and forth between Hollywood and New York. She wrote me, saying she wanted me to find her a therapist. She was hoping to see someone in LA and me when she was in NY, and I was thinking of Marilyn Monroe who did that—you know—Marianne Kris here, and Ralph Greenson there. And this is all on e-mail—she's young, and it's only e-mail and text. And so, I wrote back, trying to get her to come in. "Let's have a double session," I said, "this is a very important decision you're making, and I'm not willing to discuss it on e-mail; we need to meet." I consulted one of my friends who said, you shouldn't have written that *you were not willing* . . . And after a while, she wrote back: "just because I'm thinking of seeing someone else too? It doesn't seem like so big a deal for me, but ok." And then nothing; and a text, and then nothing. Over, and over and over. And she had always done this in terms of relationships, but I never had the time with her to point this out. At the end she wrote a termination e-mail: "I should have, I am sorry—I wish I had ended properly, I know I can't do that—that that's not the way to do things . . . but I was really great—wonderful things are happening in my life, I love you."

A: I'm thinking that today, for a lot of young people, e-mail and texting are genuine ways of relating—for you this could not have counted for a genuine relationship. You've invited her to meet her in your way and were unable to meet her in her "world"—where e-mails are more than means of making contact. For many younger people this is a relationship.

M: Maybe so, but it also serves a schizoid quality.

A: For sure, the entire culture of electronic connection is schizoid or disembodied.

M: Disembodied is a good way of putting it as what she protected herself from. On the other hand—this is apropos the patient needing to go to something else—she's done with me.

A: And you were supposed to be walking her down the aisle.

M: That's right. And certainly I've had that before. I wrote about this guy who was in treatment for a while and was unclear whether he was gay or straight. At one point when he was obsessing about it I said, "but you've never even dated a man, how would you know?" And then he started dating somebody, and began to accept his gay identity. But he also started seeing other therapists (see Dimen 2003).

A: He was dating other therapists.

M: Exactly how I put this to him. He was trying other relationships. Finally, he said, "I need to see a man and I went to some sessions to a man who does bodywork and that's what I need to do."

A: And what was it like for you?

M: Same thing: "No, no, no, wait, I'm supposed to be walking him down the aisle" . . . at the first gay wedding in his family. It was supposed to be me. The feeling . . . I think—is that an occupational hazard? You throw yourself into it in that way. You have to have that hurt, it is inevitable—and you have to have the other part of you, which is clicking along and seeing where the feeling is in that context, when they're needing you to be in that state.

A: This state sounds somewhere between Freud's (1912e) evenly hovering attention and Mitchell's (2005) allowing the patient to get under your skin, and doing it at the same time without dissociating from either.

M: Yes. There is an essay about this state by Alan Bass and Don Moss (2012). They speak more from a one-person perspective, but they are talking about the same thing, and they think of it as an erotic state. I agree: it is not a state of sexual arousal, but a state of full aliveness. The evenly hovering aspect relates to being ready for anything, a sort of a physical position like in squash, where you are open to whatever comes.

A: And again, while Ghent (1990) spoke extensively of surrender and Daniel N. Stern (2004) about the present moment, you are describing a way of being subjectively present while still holding a witnessing position—integrating a more classical psychoanalytic terminology with the mutuality of here-and-now.

M: Yes. It is mutuality *and* witnessing. There's a set of different tensions in what I'm saying, there's the evenly hovering attention and patient getting under your skin. But this is a different tension around the same thing—witnessing and mutuality, and that's pretty interesting, because witnesses are not supposed to be involved in mutual way (e.g., witnesses in Bosnia)—this is both witnessing and mutuality.

A: And the challenge is doing it non-dissociatively, and when we are unable to hold this tension it collapses into dissociative states.

M: That's what happened this morning. There's got to be a mutual dissociation going on—a projective identification. For sure, I'm holding her fury and the reason I'm acting it out is because, in part, it is not mine. Bromberg (personal communication, April 27, 1998) says that when you have a sudden affect and you are bewildered about what's going on, are asking yourself "Why do I have this feeling?"— that's projective identification. And I want to shove it back to her. She's shoving it to me. Between us we do not allow it to be in the field.

A: I am really enjoying the permission you give yourself to be aggressive.

M: Well, I can talk about it now, but perhaps part of my contribution to the enactment is my prohibition on being aggressive, in the moment. I have to have a failing that meets hers.

A: So sometimes the way of meeting is meeting our patients with our own failure.

M: Well, she's meeting me that way. I wrote about it in an essay on the body (Dimen, 2003), describing a case where I thought I've failed. Hold on, my next patient is back at the door . . . but I still have ten minutes . . . .

A:We're having a live demonstration of what we're talking about: when I cannot be met within the engagement, the periphery gets saturated with the enactment.

M: Something can't be in the relationship and then the frame gets impinged on.

An interesting angle on failure is the way that psychoanalysis makes use of them under different paradigms. Re-reading Edgar Levenson's *The Fallacy of Understanding* (1995) and *The Ambiguity of*

Change (1983), I find he identifies certain paradigms in psychoanalysis. Within them, I was wondering what would constitute failure in each of those—from a point of view of Freudians, relationists, interpersonalists? I would certainly say that enactment theory is the most recent psychoanalytic view on failure.

Enactment is something that happens in treatment. And we have a very specific tactical therapeutic meaning to it—we take something where there has been a huge mistake and we try to make use of it. Cornell (2009) gives a very good example about boundary violation in his own life, and how his analyst had betrayed him—and disclosed something about him without his permission. Cornell was very distraught, and went to talk to a trusted colleague about what had happened. His colleague, a highly experienced analyst, started to laugh, and said that such "fuck-ups" happen only when the analyst truly loves the patient. So when there is this kind of genuine love, then failure is even more inevitable.

A: I'm thinking of Stuart Pizer's (2014) generous involvement of the analyst. Perhaps what you are adding is the inevitability of owning up to our aggressive involvement, the aggressive act.

M: Yes, I think so. That's what's on my plate for Friday—with this patient, and I'd be very excited to get there . . . And now, I have to go to my next session.

A: Thank you!

M: Thank you.

CHAPTER ELEVEN

Daring anger and intimacy: clinical failure or success?*

Barbara Pizer

I begin with the assumption that the ownership of difficult affects (throughout development as well as therapy) leads to greater intimacy, creativity, and growth. One of the most challenging affects to recognise, own, and express is anger. And the case I have chosen to illustrate my point turns out, on the face of it, to be a consulting room failure! Nonetheless, there is more to this story than first meets the eye. Its outcome only redoubles my determination to tell you what I mean when I talk about the two-way track that anger may take, the potential dangers in anger disavowed, and the potential vitality that comes with ownership of anger, including the creative possibilities and risks involved in moving anger forward toward more intimate relating. But let me begin at an earlier beginning.

My mother—who held her anger back along with many other feelings—made clear that even though she loved me, I was definitely her problem child. She found me difficult to deal with. Whenever I got angry or particularly upset, I felt her disappear. And I was sure that the sudden break between us was caused by my bad behaviour. I felt deeply ashamed.

---

* For a full discussion of this written aspect of our work see Pizer, 2014.

Both in my own development and in the case I am about to describe, I explore the linking and unlinking potentials carried by anger.

From the beginning of my work in this field, my analytic sensibility has been rooted in the assumption of an innate impetus within each of us to discover or restore our own unique balance of affective cognitions. The thrust of my clinical inquiry is based on the inevitable breakdowns in cognitive–affective linking, breakdowns that hamper our thoughts about what we are feeling and interfere with the feel of whatever it is we may be thinking.

> I am reminded of myself as a young child, sitting by my mother, enjoying a satisfied feeling of pleasure as I watched her nursing my baby sister. It was as if her more usually opaque countenance had magically transformed, and I thought of her as "coming into her face". Then came the day that she was closed behind her bedroom door. I remember a bustling around me where I was just standing there nearby, not being any bother. My stomach started hurting from the now-and-then keening sounds coming from my mother's bed and muffling through the door, but I was not permitted entry. The doctor came and the doctor went. There was also a peculiar fishy aroma coming out from under the door like pickled fish mixed up with disinfectant.
>
> And when she finally came out, I noticed that she never nursed again.

I have no sensible words for this experience—only a visceral memory connected to sound and smell as well as a strong sense that my interest in breakdowns may have originated here.

Of course we realise that affective–cognitive unlinking may save us in situations of early relational trauma. We literally incapacitate ourselves for the sake of survival. But how might "survival" evolve toward re-integration and growth?

I am particularly intrigued by the ways in which the affect of anger may serve both unlinking and relinking functions. An unexpected upsurge of angry affect carries the potential to move us forward in an integrative way toward personal freedom and subsequent intimacy or may just as easily undo us, breaking off connections within ourselves as well as with others.

While pondering these ideas, I received an invitation to speak at a major conference. At the time, I was working with a woman from another country whom I greatly admired and who had entered therapy for the eight-month period of her visitor's permit. Although it seemed pretty clear that her frightening "work block" was a symptom of longer-term issues (related to some kind of early inhibition of affective expressiveness) I could not resist the opportunity to work with her. And as the time for her departure grew closer, I grew sadder that we could not move further with the task I thought we had begun so well.

Then it occurred to me that maybe I could adapt our ongoing experience as a clinical illustration for my conference paper and thereby continue our work through correspondence. I would send her drafts of what I wrote, and she would send her thoughts and comments back for me to incorporate. I felt surprised by how whole-heartedly she agreed to the project, immediately offering some fascinating inroads for consideration, and how she actually seemed vitalised by the notion that we could carry on as a team. Despite my own excitement, I did encourage discussions about the potential downsides of the venture, especially the risk of subverting our prior work. What if she came to feel exploited? She denied my apprehension and expressed rare eagerness to undertake this project, which she considered "a gift".

Now, of course, I realise that I should have thought better than to engage my patient in a collaboration by long distance instead of seeking closure to what was left of unfinished business (including our impending separation), perhaps to discover whatever we could not yet say face to face and, maybe, to move unspoken anger forward. What a breakdown between thinking and feeling processes—which is, of course, the inherent nature of enactment! Gradually, the drafts I sent her became more intermittent and her comments—although never rejecting—more circumspect. As I awaited response to my final draft, I experienced a growing apprehension that something had gone awry between us but I could not say why.

On the eve of my departure for the conference city (with final permission to give my paper not yet granted) her e-mail arrived from overseas. All bets were off. My former patient said that her identity (despite my efforts at cover-up) would still be obvious to those who knew her. Furthermore, my paper robbed her of experiences that belonged exclusively to her. I had no right to author them, even if disguised.

How could I not have foreseen this outcome? The words she used to explain her shift were polite and carefully chosen. But *her unwavering anger came through*. She expressed compassion for the position she had to put me in. However, she had no choice but to rescind permission for me to use any material related to her past experiences.

Panicked, angry, and ashamed, I arrived at the conference bearing a paper that I could not deliver.

> Only much later would I come to understand that my failures in this treatment—among them, denial of anger over our separation paired with a decided inability to recognise the disconnect it prompted— buckled us both.

But there it was and here I am. What do I do now? It is Friday evening. My presentation is Sunday morning. The title of my paper has already been printed in the programme along with the day and time allotted for presentation. The only option I can think of is to use myself as the patient. Here is an excerpt of what I said.

Even though I am no longer able to flesh out the person I planned to talk about, I believe all the more that our experience together— which she in this moment repudiates—emphasises the significance, variation, and influence of anger in human relationships, highlighted by analytic interchange.

As I become clear enough to reflect on my former patient's change of heart around my original paper, I see that, in a way, her withdrawal could not legitimately be called a part of analytic interchange. (*She is out of reach and I must realise she is not my mother*). At best, I have to take responsibility for having created an enactment without a context to contain it. Looking back I can see that my own personal grief over the arbitrary loss of our connection had a lot to do with the wish to set down something of my view of what transpired between us. A way of holding.

The central issue around which I believed our work revolved and around which this paper still revolves has to do with anger, intimacy, and the release of creative freedom as these factors apply to analytic work. I believe that genuine intimacy between patient and analyst is dependent on the ability of *both partners* to trust their ongoing process, with trust being contingent on the degree to which each participant can recognise, metabolise, and ultimately express angry emotions directly to one another.

For me, the therapeutic work and play lies in finding common pathways that lead toward an acceptable degree of intimacy between participants. Analytic intimacy begins with the analyst's ability to be

anger intimacy & creative expression freedom

herself as analyst, to discover moment-by-moment who that self is in relation to each patient and to be with what each patient brings to the interaction (see Russell, 1996). As I define it, this kind of intimacy between analyst and patient takes its own sweet time, is neither preordained nor static but rather a genuinely felt ongoing back and forth, a moment-by-moment negotiation of closeness and distance. Intimate analytic relating in this asymmetrical context involves the gradual achievement of mutual engagement, including the ability to recognise and metabolise angry emotions. Somewhere inside, both parties in the analytic enterprise will know that trust between them remains contingent until they have each expressed and received exchanges directly and consciously fuelled by anger, and together lived through its shared experience. Above all else, the process takes time.

My ire rises as I think now about my former patient, who seems to consider the paper I wrote as an insult when I thought it was a document in which my warmth, my foibles, and empathic caring came through as did our mutual efforts to make sense of her dilemma. She is furious, the kind of fury that frightens me, the kind that leaves me feeling three years old and wanting to appease.

But then again, why is it that we analysts so often forget about transference dynamics—working both ways I hasten to add—when we feel we are being so "authentic"! Or maybe the way in which we think we are being real is actually thoughtless, hurtful, judgmental, bullying, inattentive.

> I can remember like yesterday that freezing winter afternoon when fifth grade let out, and the class bully, Alice, suddenly grabbed hold of me from behind and pushed me down on my knees and rubbed my face in the snow. I can remember running home crying, to tell my mother, sobbing that Alice pushed me in the snow—to which my mother coolly replied, "And what did you do to her?"

For me, the track of my emotional reactions usually moves from hurt and anger to shame and hurt, and then in rapid fire, to the rescue, I design an angry fantasy that gets me back up on my feet again.

Hopefully for analyst or therapist, the process of acknowledging her anger—while aware of her powerful role in the dyad—initially takes the form of an internal negotiation or conversation. I believe that the patient will pick up the analyst's implicit struggles and make of them what she can bear at the time. And, one can hope, in her good time, the patient will begin to feel safe enough to express what she feels directly to the analyst, including her anger. And here I risk the statement that genuine trust cannot be fully attained without identifying, engaging, working through, and surviving direct expressions fuelled by anger and together lived through its shared experience. A responsive upsurge of anger may become a clarifying signal in a relationship, a statement of personal boundary that defines for the other the degree of closeness or distance permitted in this particular moment.

Is it not ironic then, that my former patient's responses to me that came out of a draft I sent her (purported understanding that morphed in cyberspace into misunderstanding both ways) led to expressions of anger between us now that neither of us could fully feel *in vivo*? We missed the freedom that we both had wished for, the creative freedom that just might have been. If only we had had the time!

Makes me mad. "I'm rubber, you're glue," I am thinking to tell my former patient now, "Whatever you say, jumps off of me and sticks to you."

Almost immediately, I turn myself around. "This is hubris. All your fault." I am hugely ashamed. Now to the whole world at large, "You know what she said," I parrot on, "she said, 'you didn't listen—you seem to have been thinking about yourself all the time'." And I turn around again. "But I'm all I have left, dumbbell, now that you took yourself away, you can just go jump in a lake!"

I know that when my feelings move in that direction, I am sunk if I let them go down. The internal landscape is barren and familiar. Under it all I feel "caught out", ashamed beyond belief, maybe for having set the whole thing up in the first place, so all I can do is blather diatribes inside my head to muster up the energy that anger provides. Some energy to pull myself together.

Clearly anger comes in various flavours and may help or hinder whatever it is we wish for in our lives; anger may be growth producing, creative, protective, defensive, or destructive. Although we know that all of us are born with the capacity to feel, *owning* whatever the feeling is that wells up inside is something else entirely. Recognition, acceptance, and creative use of one's anger may be one of our most difficult developmental tasks.

Once more I am reminded of my mother's comment when Alice took me down. Perhaps the consequence of receiving automatic and unjust blame is that it feeds the idea that anger must be "justified" before one has "a right", to feel it. And then what follows may be the insidious merger of anger with judgment that sends a person so far away from spontaneity and trust that should you happen to ask her what she is feeling, she will shrug and tell you, "nothing". And soon she will believe it, experiencing nothing at all or something else. Some degree of trust must be established before patient (or therapist) dares to test her anger in an analytic setting. Most likely it works both ways. Just as the affects of love and hate bear a close relationship with one another, so too may anger and trust.

Although I realise that this focus on inner process right now relates only to me, I hope it has relevance to you as well. I see that even though I hold myself responsible for having caused my former patient anguish, I am separating, slowly, from her global assessment.

I do remember sitting with her on a winter day, talking deeply about a history of growing up that left her with the kind of scars that maybe one could overcome to some degree, make some creative use of their enduring ache (and is that not what we as therapists routinely do, what makes us therapists in the first place?), but scars that just will never go away. I can feel the way it was as we sat together enveloped in a long silence. I was filled with a mixture of experience for which I had no words, perhaps because my own reveries had fallen away. The way I felt with her was a way I had not felt before—a depth of pain that could just as easily have flopped over into joy, a very quiet and connected place where—as in dreams—opposite feelings intertwine, a timeless place. Outside my window it had just begun to snow—thick random flakes.

Even if today she will deny it ever happened, even if the thing is only a figment of my imagination, even if I need it as a source of solace, I can feel it inside, and it belongs to me—next to my anger and my sadness and whatever else there is.

And now I have arrived at a new place. I recognise that anger is more than just a feeling. Anger may also be a mode of transportation that carries with it a richness of unexpected feelings as it travels along, feelings and combinations of feelings never experienced in quite this way before or again. I also realise that anger, like laughter, may move us out of dissociation and into the present moment.

My former patient sees me in a line up with the other figures who betrayed her, and that makes me feel *shut out*. But if the paper triggered my patient, then maybe I need to take it personally in the sense

anger – moves one out of dissociation

that I may not be its object, but I do, in a way, need to stand alongside her line up of perpetrators. I feel sad and responsible for that.

As I go over my notes about the work with my former patient, I still believe that together we touched her anger as well as mine, her pain as well as mine. But we did not have the time to hold it long enough in the room between us for her to metabolise it in the present. Whether my former patient will ever forgive me or ever completely "get" what I am trying to articulate is an open question. I have no idea what or how much she will ultimately hang on to from the limited time we spent. As for my experience, I can say without a doubt that a dimension of feeling has opened in me that had not been there before, a feeling as real and as evanescent as the first fall of snow outside my office window.

Postscript

I knew I would show my former patient how her anger with me worked for me. Our angry exchange did not destroy either of us, but her anger carried enough potency to influence and bring about change. The new version of my paper honoured her objections, and I sent it off to her right away.

In contrast to the preceding fiasco, my former patient replied almost immediately. She appreciates my paper, finds it "courageous". The powerful directness she invests in her lengthy e-mail arguments strikes me as a familiar aspect of who she is and was, but when she sat with me in person, I felt it only as a shadow. Or shadows, I should say. This new version of my paper apparently evoked the coming out of her separate self-states all together in a single document. I get a glimpse of her gratitude, disdain, appreciation, reproach, and global self-criticism, discrete awareness of self and other, and awareness of that as "progress". But sadly, there is no one "standing in the spaces" (Bromberg, 1998) with her as she releases these parts of self, that make simultaneous appearances in the same e-mail like orphans taking issue in a play of words.

My former patient writes directly about her anger with me. "This time," she writes, "I thought about it hard and tried to say clearly what I was angry about." And, "I thought this change in my behaviour was a sign of progress."

Concluding her e-mail, my former patient writes, "I came to you in the first place because I could not work . . . . And you kept telling me I'd start soon. That didn't happen. But after I expressed my anger about your [first] paper, something changed." And then, she lets me know that even before receiving my revision, "I intended to e-mail and tell you that I started working again."

PART V

BROADER PERSPECTIVES

Introduction to Part V

I n this last section we shall introduce some broader contexts through which to examine failure. We shall look at *when* is failure rather than *what* is failure. Psychotherapy takes place in culture, it is always political (Samuels, 2006; Totton, 2000) and should be explored and judged with its background in mind.

Joseph Schwartz honestly self-examines his working life as a psychotherapist through the lens of outcomes, attempting to understand some failures, to accept others, and to still ponder about others. Nancy Eichhorn brings a case study that ended her career as a therapist before it could begin, bringing up the question of the holding environment and the necessary conditions for providing good-enough psychotherapy. It also questions the actual possibility of learning from our mistakes in a culture dominated by accountability and fears of litigation (Rolef Ben-Shahar, 2007; Totton, 2006). Next, Julianne Appel-Opper introduces intercultural perspectives that impact the therapeutic act and again examines the necessary and sufficient conditions for the therapist's ability to feel at home and offer a home to her clients. Last, Asaf Rolef Ben-Shahar looks at the characterological potential and risk in the therapeutic personality. Examining the masochistic aspect of the therapeutic profession, he wonders about the possibility of healing our own wounds as psychotherapists while practicing psychotherapy.

CHAPTER TWELVE

An informal account of therapeutic outcomes in one practice of psychotherapy over a twenty year period

Joseph Schwartz

Introduction

When I was doing a post-doctorate course at the New York Psychiatric Institute in New York, I learned a valuable lesson about success and failure from the medical students on the programme. They were very careful about using the words success and failure because medicine, like psychotherapy, is a tricky business. The human organism is too complex to offer simple generalisations about how things work. Instead, they would quote what was apparently an old saying in medical education: "I supply the treatment. God supplies the cure." I take this to mean for psychotherapy that there are unknowables in treating mental pain through the talking cure. But I do think we can make some approximate judgements about who we think we have helped in psychotherapy, specifically whether the client has done the work on themselves that needed to be done.

Outcomes and the talking cure

I would distinguish three somewhat different areas to evaluate outcomes. Simply put there is the outcome of the intake interview(s), the outcome in short-term work of up to two years, and the outcome in long term work of over two years. I will try to follow Asaf Ben-Shahar's advice to evaluate outcomes in my work in the three areas losing neither rigour nor self-kindness.

Outcomes of intake interviews

A client may not return after one, two, or three initial interviews. The reasons for the failure to take up therapy with me are sometimes known, sometimes not. Two clients said to me that they could not see me because I lived in too big a house. Class consciousness can be very high in the UK. Another client left after two sessions because he felt therapy was not going to help him with how strongly sexed he felt, and when he felt he needed sex it was okay to pay for it. A third case, a woman suffering the bereavement of the loss of her mother described in vivid detail how her mother killed herself by drowning herself in the sea. The pain was intense and I was moved to tears. This served to anger the woman who said she did not come to therapy to have to watch someone else's pain. I thought this was fair comment and worked in supervision to try to minimise the risk of re-traumatisation in therapy.

Others simply failed to appear at a scheduled time and did not respond to a follow up note. It is easy enough to say the potential client was too closed, not ready for therapy, and refused the offered treatment. In such short encounters, however, it can be difficult to understand what did not work. In one case, a man had come to therapy in order to work through an extremely painful ending of his relationship involving the loss of his two children. Right at the end of the session I said, "you've described a very painful ending but I think you've held back your feelings. I don't think the two of us have connected." He said he felt the same way and was glad I had brought it up. The two of us did work together effectively for the next two years. But it is not always possible to sense a lack of connection in a first session. Quite the opposite in that it can feel very connected. In that case we can guess that it is the deeply avoidant client who does not return precisely because the connection has been experienced as too frightening.

There are cases where one session is good enough (in a Winnicottian sense). A woman came to see me suffering the still-birth of her first child. Her husband, her relatives, and her close friends were saying, "Don't cry, you can always have another." I strongly felt her grief in the room and said, "You are entitled to grieve this loss. Try not to let them talk you out of it. It might take as long as a year to heal." This was a case, as Bowlby has emphasised, where mourning was nature's way to heal loss. My client breathed a long sigh and said: "Thank you so much. This is what I needed to hear."

Outcomes of long-term work

The words success and failure are not quite rich enough to describe outcomes in long term work. But how do we sense when a therapy is finished?

I think there can be a sense that the client has completed the work they came into therapy to do. Both client and therapist can feel it: we have come to an ending. And in the context of endings, perhaps it can be said that the therapy has been a success if it is clear (enough) that the client has completed the work he or she came into therapy to do.

But nothing is quite that simple. One client came into therapy for help in managing a painful divorce. He had taken the step of divorcing his wife with great pain because he had been committed to standing by her no matter what. He felt he had betrayed that commitment. In addition, he had a teenaged son who he was afraid of losing. He had been a very active engaged father and his ex-wife was leaving London to return to her home town in the north of England taking their son with her. My client was in a lot of pain. We worked through his feelings of needing/feeling obligated to look after his wife stemming from being a parental child, and he was able to establish a satisfactory relationship with his son even with the distance. There were many issues along the way including transitional class issues and problems in forming a new relationship.

After three years, the work seemed to be done. I suggested to him that he had accomplished what he wanted to do—to free himself from guilt over leaving his wife, guilt about re-marrying, and to solve the problem of how to continue his relationship with his son at a distance. He was not having it. I could not understand his reluctance to leave. He just said "I'm not ready". I waited, not pushing the issue. Something was going on.

Finally, after about a year of not much happening in his therapy except accounts of how well things were working out both in his new relationship, with his son, and with his family of origin including his mother, he came in one day and said "My wife has found me out." I did not suspect an affair. It just was not in his character. What was it?

His wife had taken a close look at their finances and discovered that there was a spend of about thirty pounds a week unaccounted for. It had then come out. My client had a drinking problem. Every day before coming home from work he went to a pub and had two or three pints. He promised his wife to stop and had immediately enrolled in a twelve-step programme.

I had not suspected it except for his reluctance to end. The transitional class tensions he experienced at work in his job as a successful screenwriter seemed to require a daily comforting pub experience before going home. He dealt with his need for the comfort of the pub by giving up the pints and ordering water or juice. He explored at length about how highly he valued his hands-on working class background, feeling it superior to the elitist middle class know-nothings he encountered working in film. I have warm feelings for this man. There was an authenticity, competence, and thoughtfulness to him that I found very appealing.

In this case there was no beating myself up about my not recognising whatever clues he may have given about his pub experience. I have found that surprises are so routine in our work that very little leads to self-recrimination or to feelings of having been deceived. I did wonder whether, as a transitional-class American, in spite of living for thirty years in Britain, I was not sufficiently alert to the hidden injuries of class in the UK. Perhaps I was not. A lack of direct experience is an occupational hazard for every psychotherapist. It is in the nature of the work to not have first-hand experience of the client's life.

What about long term work, when the therapy has to end, not because the work has been accomplished, but because it has not?

One theme that appears in work with clients for whom the therapy is not working is a consistent use of the words: "Yes, but . . ." (Muller, 2010). A man I saw for three and a half years had survived violent abuse by his father. He had entered therapy because of difficulties with money. He was the oldest of three sons, and his mother was overburdened by an absent husband, always at work, and charged with the responsibility of raising the three children. My client appeared to his mother to be wild and out of control. Examples seemed to be, on the surface, rather mild as in my client riding his bike with no hands, taking what seemed to me to be the ordinary risks that boys take growing up. His mother, however, in her attempt to discipline her oldest boy, would say: "Wait until I tell your father. He'll put you right."

The result was that my client would lie awake at night in terror listening for his father's footsteps as he, fuelled by rage stoked by my client's mother, came up to give him a beating. When I offered the observation that his father was not only absent but abusive, my client would say: "Yes, but . . ." He might say, "I admire my father. He was strong." His money problems involved spending more on housing and holidays than he could afford. He worked as an IT specialist but did not earn enough to adequately cover the cost of holidays to Thailand or to cover the mortgage on his house in Camden. He could not accept the possibility of moving quarters, or to taking less expensive holidays, saying, "Yes but, I've always dreamed of owning my own house."

Towards the end of our relationship, I began to insist to him that "Yes, but. . ." was not good enough. He needed to begin to look at how traumatic his childhood was, including the collusion and the approval of his mother with the abuse that his father visited on him. The result was that my client left to take a job in New York. He said he had begun to feel threatened when coming to therapy. He did not feel safe. I agreed that the work was making him feel unsafe and could not be undertaken at this time.

It is not possible to know whether this first attempt at therapy may have paved the way for a therapist in NY to work effectively with him later. Possibly. A second or third therapist always has it easier. But in this therapy, it is hard not to draw the conclusion that the work that needed to be done was not done. And I did blame myself. What had I not seen or understood in the "yes, buts . . ."? His work was not done, thwarted by "yes, buts . . ." that would not/could not yield.

Finally, in long term work, I think there is something to say about the exceptionally long term client. I have a client who is just completing her therapy after fifteen years. She is a survivor of organised childhood sexual abuse. As a therapist who completed a partially classical training, I am very conscious of Freud's famous paper "Analysis terminable and interminable" (1937c). But in cases of extreme trauma as in childhood chronic childhood sexual abuse and torture, I have found that the book needs to be revised. All my very long-term clients were sufferers of complex trauma and dissociation.

Outcomes in work lasting from two months to two years

In short term work it might develop that the client discovered that he or she did not want to do the work after all. One client, who complained bitterly in session after session about the difficulties in her life, said: "I just want to talk. Who else am I going to find to talk to?"

If there were to be a common theme in the short-term work that did not accomplish the work that the client came into therapy to do, it might be that the client discovered that he or she could not or would not do the work they came to do. If I ask myself what my part as the therapist plays in these cases, I would say that perhaps I do not relate to the avoidant client with enough determination. For example, I always refer a male client on if they have been sent by their wives. I do not have the patience and determination to accomplish work that needs to be done when the clients themselves have not come of their own accord. On the other hand, however, I find that cases of OCD, which many colleagues avoid, seem to bring strong feelings into the room so that it is possible to address the emotional conflict that leads to the compulsive behaviour.

Conclusion

A discussion of success and failure is arguably just the bare beginning of the extremely difficult project of assessing outcome. Outcome is a problem that has plagued the talking cure from its inception in Freud's house in the Bergasse (Schwartz, 1999). If we take a dynamic point of view, every success and failure has its own deeper meanings. But it is also true, as Rolef Ben-Shahar and Shalit (this volume) emphasise, that success and failure are rarely explored in trainings or after:

> We are taught about attachment, about rupture and repair, but neither about the pain of failing to help a client, nor about unrecoverable alliance ruptures and the guilt or shame that might accompany these. As a result we are afraid to make mistakes—and frequently remain paralysed, shamed and silent about those professional stepping stones. (p. 1)

We might note that for experienced clinicians, it may not be a fear of making mistakes, but the fear of writing about them. And this is because in our present culture it is not safe enough to acknowledge therapies that fail, that do not accomplish the work that the client came to do. The talking cure has too many professional and public enemies for any of us to feel safe, whether consciously or not, in publically discussing difficulties and limitations in the talking cure. But I also want to report an observation of Peter Fonagy that compared to chronic cases in medicine, psychotherapy can claim a long term success rate of around fifty per cent compared to thirty-three per cent in chronic cases in medicine (Fonagy, 2002).

My colleagues have persuaded me that it may not be useful to speak in terms of success and failure because any outcome is a result of dynamic processes that need to be analysed and understood. Nevertheless, I will try to make some kind of conclusion about my practice.

First, I think it is useful to define failure as a failure of the client–therapist couple working together to accomplish the work the client came to do. In this light, it would seem that failing to take up therapy after intake or to continue therapy in short term work is associated with a refusal, inability, or fear of facing the challenge of the work. There can be irrevocable ruptures as in re-traumatisation, themselves of dynamic origin, which end the therapeutic possibilities. And in the intake situation all too frequently there can be little chance of addressing the barrier(s) that prevent an initial connection between client and therapist.

I believe long term work is too varied for any simple generalisation. Perhaps it could be said that in long term work an entanglement can develop that cannot be addressed effectively, which eventually exhausts the therapeutic relationship.

I remain with considerable uncertainty about how outcomes of the psychotherapeutic relationship are to be discussed let alone assessed. But I do agree with the editors that a failure to address these problems in trainings and in our journals is a failure that weakens our field.

CHAPTER THIRTEEN

We met in borrowed space

Nancy Eichhorn

W e met in a colleague's office, the windows framed silky black cormorants perched on rocks to dry their feathers. Tidal waters eddied around feathers of rime ice on this December morn.

Walter entered; a tentative tone in his poise and pace. He had a noticeable limp; he favoured his right leg. His eyes darted from me to the window to the love seat to the easy chair, which was positioned to afford adequate space and eye contact between the room's occupants. Walter removed his knit cap and winter coat, snowflakes littered the carpet. I motioned toward the coat rack; he obliged.

"Thank you again for seeing me," Walter said. He reached out to shake my hand; the hesitancy in his eyes clarified the action as one of social etiquette not one of personal choice.

"You're welcome Walter. I appreciate your willingness to work with a student in training. Please, take a seat."

Walter stood an instant longer. His skeletal frame struggled to provide the framework necessary to shape his button-up cotton shirt and faded blue jeans. He perched on the edge of the couch. Feet together. Hands on his lap.

We met at the request of a colleague, who I will call Wilma. She and I worked together at a mental health agency where I was hired for per diem work. She was a licensed marital and family therapist working in the child and adolescent sector. Wilma knew I was currently immersed in my Basic Level 1 Eye Movement and Desensitization and Reprocessing Therapy (EMDR) training and that I needed supervised hours to complete my certification. Walter, she explained, was injured at his job site, but he was off-duty at the time; he did not have medical insurance nor was workmen's compensation offered. He suffered flashbacks, insomnia, and social isolation. He was unable to return to work.

His nine-year-old son, George, was Wilma's client. Walter's mental state impacted George's state of being; neither were doing well. Wilma assured me that Walter was stable, not suicidal. He just needed someone to help him; she felt EMDR was the perfect solution—a few finger waves, release some sensations stored in the amygdala, and off he would go back to work. I called my EMDR supervisor, who lived in another state. He said, sure, it all sounded fine. It was almost Christmas vacation, however, and I was set to travel out-of-state for two weeks. I asked if the first appointment could wait until January.

"No," Wilma said, a tone of insistence in her voice. "Walter needs to meet with you as soon as possible—for George's sake. Any movement in a positive direction will make their Christmas all the better."

I knew better than to rush things, but I felt compelled to help. And I was eager to start the EMDR process with a "real" client, to put my fledgling skills to use in a true life case rather than practice sessions with colleagues also training in EMDR. I envisioned meeting Walter and teaching him some skills to ensure a joyous Christmas. I thought we could approach the more serious work healing the past trauma and its influence on his quality of life when I returned. It seemed like a win-win situation: Walter gets support, Wilma is happy with me for helping, and I gain real life experience. Everyone's needs, in my mind, were going to be met.

It is simple to delude oneself. To play the role of hero when you sense people need to be rescued. I had already learned as a teacher that caring too much actually created dependency and disempowered students; the best course was to offer skills with love and compassion, and then stand aside and let them work out their own situations and live with the consequences of their choices. I was not supposed to swoop into their lives and make everything better. Why I thought EMDR was different than teaching escapes me. I honestly believed that EMDR was the cure for Walter's emotional troubles. As no one else was willing to help Walter, I believed it was up to me to make it happen.

Session One

Walter and I sat opposite one another. We had spoken on the phone and established the guidelines: I was a student training in EMDR; I was under supervision; I was doing this pro bono in exchange for his time. I reiterated my credentials; he said he understood and that he was desperate to end these flashbacks and get his life back. We only had time for two sessions before the holiday so I did not want to get into anything heavy. Walter, however, worked on a different timeline.

I held my clipboard with the appropriate EMDR forms. The client history included his current concern (presenting complaint) and any related experiences that may have occurred in the past. From here we were to develop a target sequence plan for memory reprocessing.

Step one: Presenting Complaint

"Now let's talk about the problem you have decided to focus on today. What are the present experiences causing the disturbance/symptoms/reactions that you are experiencing?" I asked.

Walter explained that he was involved in an accident at work—a forklift, laden with boxes, pinned him against wall; the end of the metal fork severed his upper thigh, sliced through skin, muscle, tendon, bone. He limped now but considering the original prognosis of amputation, well, he felt blessed. However, he could not return to the job site. Anytime he heard truck-like sounds or saw equipment related to his job at the loading platform he froze. He wanted to forget his fear and get back to work. His family depended on his income, his son no longer respected him, and his wife had moved out months ago. He wanted to dive right in and get going.

We agreed to meet the following week. I explained that as a student I was sharing his story with my supervisor and had him sign the appropriate release forms. I also received permission to research insurance options for him. I felt positive about our first session. Walter was quiet and yet self-reflective. He knew what he wanted, was clear about his values, and he was willing to do the work to heal and bring his life back together.

Session Two

Walter arrived agitated, distracted, intense. Sight and smell signalled he had not showered for several days nor changed his clothes; I doubt he had eaten much either. Trucks were haunting him, he said. He wanted out of his nightmare, now. It was almost Christmas and his son was going to spend the holidays with his mom (soon to be Walter's ex-wife). He faced two weeks alone. I felt his intensity, and I felt my fear. This was not the same man I had met the week before. His desperation outdistanced my skill as a new therapist. I had worked with children during the past year whose worst case scenarios were depression and anger and sexual abuse. While these are not simple life experiences, they did not come close to Walter's overarching hopelessness and helplessness. But, I felt committed; no one else opted to help Walter and now he counted on me. What had I done?

Per EMDR protocol, I explained how memory worked and that a high level of emotion may occur while reprocessing memories. We needed to develop a calm/safe place where he could retreat to when he felt overwhelmed both in the session and on his own—resourcing was a necessary stabilisation skill along with relaxation and stress reduction we learned in Level 1. My trainer had stressed the immense need for the client to have a workable means of dissipating a disturbance if necessary during or between sessions; I was mandated to practice creating a calm/safe place as a precursor to the actual EMDR session. Within this process, I was taught to discuss negative *vs.* positive cognitions. A positive self-concept was one of our goals as well as to establish adequate life supports and to call for help if necessary.

Trust is one of the essential elements in any therapeutic relationship, is it not? I wanted Walter to know that I trusted him, and I wanted to project the image of competence—that I knew what I was doing when in fact I did not. My gut felt queasy, something felt off. I referenced photocopied guide sheets—step 1, step 2. Despite my hesitation, we moved forward to the Preparation Steps with one caveat: Walter agreed to practice the mechanics of the EMDR process using a safe calming thought *vs.* a negative belief or thought as directed in the manual. We went through the proper sitting position, the correct distance between us, and the sequence of eye movements—bilateral stimulation and movement type: one for stabilising and resource development (slow, four to eight passes) and the other for reprocessing (fast, twenty-four or more passes). It felt mechanical to me, nothing felt intuitive or known. When working with children at the clinic, I sensed into the moment and trusted what came. I did not need a guidebook to walk me through the motions. What needed to happen, just happened.

We started with an image of a calm place. He offered hugging his son. He visualised George, felt into George's presence, smelled his freshly washed hair, his downy freshened pyjamas warm from the dryer. Tears came, slow at first, then fast, hard, a flood. He cried out, "I want to die. Please dear God, let me die!" Then he froze. Nothing. No sound, no movement, no eye flicker, no breath. I was frozen, too.

"Walter? Walter can you hear me?"

He blinked. "I'm so sorry, I didn't mean anything I said. I don't want to die. I haven't tried to kill myself for months now."

I gulped. Wilma had said he had never been suicidal and here he was fully presenting with a suicidal background and a current plea to die.

"Walter, our time is almost over, and I'm concerned about you. We need to make a plan so you'll be safe for yourself and for your son."

"Yes, yes, George needs me, I know. I miss my wife. I don't want to be alone." Walter's words were garbled, laden with tears and grief.

The pressure to go ahead, when Walter's intensity screamed for more practiced intervention, overwhelmed me. I was terrified. Sitting alone with Walter in my colleague's office, I had created an island without supervision or support. I could not simply excuse myself, leave the room, and seek help. I trusted Wilma's presentation of Walter's needs. And I had worked as an independent instructor for so long that I falsely believed I had the foundational skills to go alone. I was unprepared for what occurred and felt cornered in the moment. I could not just say, "Sorry Walter, this is wrong. We have to stop and you have to leave. Sorry you don't have any health insurance and there's no one else out there to help you. But I cannot help you either." I felt forced to move forward. If I abandoned him in this moment, I was not sure what he would do.

I explained that I had made an appointment for him at a non-profit mental health agency after the holidays and that he needed someone to meet with regularly, a therapist who was trained and licensed to do the work he needed. He balked. I heard him and did my best to support him while reiterating that I was only a student, that I was not qualified to work with him, to offer him the kind of support he needed. My body shook; my voice quivered. I wanted to run away. I wanted to stop this moment, end this experience. What had I done?

Then, we wrote a suicide contract. Handwritten. Pure, clean. A stop gap. My EMDR supervisor said I did the right thing considering the situation and agreed that I needed to step away.

I got the call a week later. My former supervisor at the clinic, who I will call Ray, explained that Walter arrived at the local ER on Christmas Eve in bad shape. He noted on the intake form that he was only there because he promised his therapist that he would not do anything drastic, that he would come for help before it was too late. When asked for his therapist's name he replied, Nancy Eichhorn.

"When you get back, there will be a meeting with our administration," Ray said. Then he added, "What were you thinking? How could you do this to me?" His fury was flammable. He had been accused of improper conduct for allowing me to work with Walter, of which he had no idea that Wilma had asked me and that I accepted. Ray, who was not my EMDR supervisor, was not privy to the conversations I had with my EMDR trainer via Skype.

I arrived at the clinic an hour early per Ray's instructions. The meeting lasted all of thirty seconds. Clean out your office space. Your clients have been reassigned to other therapists. I have not worked as a psychotherapist since.

The administrator left. I tried to speak, but Ray's anger prevented him from hearing me explain that I had made a drastic mistake, that I had trusted Wilma (who it turns out was no longer an employee there), and that at least, thank God, Walter honoured the suicide contract and was alive and in care. "It was a mistake," I said. "I am just starting out. Isn't there room for learning from our mistakes?" My words fell hard on deaf ears.

Nor did it matter that my clients, ages five to eighteen, who had attachment and abandonment concerns, who relied on rage and self-abuse for outlets, who were raped, beaten, drugged, bullied, and more, were once again left by someone they had trusted and revealed their most sacred vulnerabilities to be witnessed with love and healed in a loving relationship. I never knew what they were told.

I slunk out into the heavy snow blanketing the walkway, the world shroud in crystalline white. The beauty escaped me. I shrunk into guilt, grief, anger. Confusion boggled my vision, my mind. I was numb. What had I done?

In Retrospect

Had I told Ray about Wilma's request, he might have explained the ramifications and legalities of working long distance with a supervisor, in an office isolated and alone, with no recourse should something arise beyond my ability. He might have saved me from making a tragic mistake that ended my brief career as a therapist.

Had I not heard Walter, not seen him and felt into him, he might have died that Christmas Eve (I have no information about him or any of my former clients). I had to learn the hard way that while I was accomplished as a teacher, as a writer, as an editor, I was not a practiced therapist, and I was not ready to clean-up all of the world's mental and emotional spills. My role in this life has been that of a leader, a doer, a mover. I make things happen that no one else can. Take charge and go forth. "I am a rock. I am an island." These attitudes do not fly in a team environment—whether the team is a client and myself or a client and a cadre of health care workers.

I admit it was difficult to write this. What will you, the reader, think? How will I be judged? Who will see the fear within the strength and understand my need to pick up the stray ends when no one else in the system was willing to work with Walter? There is always a risk when you write your truth, when you face the reality of your experience. No one wants to see themselves as less than, as a failure. I was raised to strive for perfection. And the truth is, this is not my first failed experience in life, and it will not be the last.

While writing, I revisited these scenes again and again. First I saw where I failed myself. Brilliant flashing neon lights surrounded my failure—it was all about me and my inability. I felt the harsh incrimination of my ego and my drive to save the world, one client at a time. I held my breath when I wrote about the choices I made so confidently as if I could truly save Walter from the demons locked in his flashbacks. I saw me, the conqueror, who believes she can assume any task and complete it successfully. And then, in each subsequent revision, I began to see where the system failed me as well. I made a mistake and there was no room for error. I was let go immediately with no chance to learn from the experience. I honestly thought my supervisor at the clinic would be more forgiving. I thought we could process the events that transpired so I might be a better person and a more capable therapist. Left alone with my mistake left me alone in the field of psychotherapy, with nowhere to turn. My EMDR supervisor explained they had to fire me. The administrator had to protect the clinic from any potential lawsuit or responsibility. It was the way of clinics and politics.

Indeed, I made many mistakes, and accept the enactment of my own history with Walter; I, too, became dissociative and acted into his dissociative pattern. But one could say there was an organisational collusion with the dissociation as well. It started with Wilma's despair of needing her client's dad to be supported and knowing he had no insurance. There was no space for repairing the therapeutic enactment (Hirsch, 1993), which points to two important factors that deserve attention here: first, a culture dominated by threats of liability and litigation inhibits and sometimes prevents working through ruptures. Second, offering therapy to people outside the system (those without insurance), who are oftentimes those needing therapy most, is not only discouraged but also punished.

Notwithstanding my own wrongdoings, which I have taken responsibility for, and in a professional sense paid heavily for, Ray's fear of litigation made him collapse our space into doer–done dynamics (Benjamin, 2004). I wonder how possible it is to practice psychotherapy freely when the student and practitioner are so unprotected—when accountability precedes responsibility; when fear is used to control our practice (Bloom, 2006).

And I am also left wondering about Walter, the uninsured man: an untouchable. If people like Walter pose such a threat to the system, what chance do they stand of getting help? What happens when psychotherapy is only offered to those who can afford it? Disorganised attachment, trauma and abuse often result in people like Walter—unable to pay, left to their own device, where nobody wants to know anything about them, with little hope.

Staring into my own reflection at this point, I am glad I wrote this story, glad I can share my failure with others so that errors can be viewed as a part of the whole of a human life and not some streak of sickness to be ostracised from our reality. Life involves risks, and there is no way to count on the outcome when it comes to interpersonal relationships. We cannot predict how people will respond to our approach, to our intervention, to our presence in their life. And yet, if we can count on forgiveness, if we can count on compassion, if we can count on love, we can greet our clients with our eyes wide open, with our minds receptive, with our bodies awakened to resonate with the other person before us and trust that what occurs is meant to happen and what transpires will be for the greater good.

And if something happens that we cannot comprehend, it would be refreshing to know someone is there to stand beside us, to guide us, to offer us insight and ideas. Therapy is not meant to happen in seclusion. It is not a single person meeting another. It occurs within a community as we enter into relationships with our clients and with our colleagues, to create a foundation from which we can all grow.

CHAPTER FOURTEEN

Failures, challenges, and learning within the field of intercultural psychotherapy, supervision, and training

Julianne Appel-Opper

I n this chapter I look closely into the challenges of intercultural psychotherapy, supervision, and training. I will draw from relational psychoanalytical and dialogical gestalt psychotherapy thinking. With the concepts of field theory and field conditions I shall deconstruct my experiences of having lived and worked for nine years in the UK, and then moved back to Germany.

The culture-blind therapist in her own field

The scenario that the therapist comes from the main/dominant culture and the client is the foreigner in the room is quite common in texts about intercultural psychotherapy. Authors like Dhillon-Stevens (2012) or Sperry (2012) point us to the danger of enacting the dyad's culturally embedded assumption that the foreigner—the other—will assimilate.

At the start of my clinical work, in the late 1980s and early 1990s, the concept of cultural difference stayed out of the psychosomatic clinics I had worked in Germany. I became fascinated by the non-verbal behaviour, how tiny bodily movements would convey stories that were not spoken as words. I was well supported by the medical director of the clinic and had the space to experiment and to find creative ways to work with a body-focus with my patients. In finding my professional home I co-created a field, in which I felt supported and respected, quite contrary to my experiences in my family of origin.

The migrant therapist . . .

There are a growing number of texts that describe intercultural psychotherapy from a relational perspective in which the therapist's subjectivity finds a valid space (e.g., Hill, 2008; Kogan, 2007; Walsh, 2014). Most of these authors had immigrated themselves. It seems as if their culture and race and their felt otherness could not be excluded in the consulting room.

Sapriel and Palumbo (2001) share how their perception and understanding had been culturally coloured in. Lobban (2013) describes how she identifies with her client's foreign boyfriend: "appointing herself as his cultural consultant" (p. 560), explaining him to her "American insider" client. Working through this enactment both therapist and client in their own space could recognise their exiled facets of themselves. Lobban adds how she had tried to keep her pile of "South African" selves rigidly separated from her "American selves" and how processing her feelings of this "double consciousness" her sense of "me-ness expanded". Within this frame, authors define culture as "the way the world is" (Wheeler, 2005, p. 47) or "the air that one breathes" (Tömmel, 2010, p. 97).

I left Germany because my husband had been offered a position in the UK. Yes, I took my culture with me into my psychotherapeutic work in the UK and with this, also the implicit cultural knowledge of how to be in my professional reality. I took the experience with me of having worked from a big, airy consulting room at a psychosomatic clinic. I remember vividly the first client when I started to work in my own private practice in the UK. I had arranged to see clients at a psychotherapy centre in which I booked a consulting room at an hourly rate. On this morning, the only room left available was the smallest room in the centre giving space for two chairs and a small table. I recall feeling like an elephant in a tiny porcelain shop in which I could not breathe. Interestingly, I do not recall any of the content the

British woman and I, the German therapist, had spoken in this first session. She did not contact me again, which fed my doubts whether I was able to offer psychotherapy in a different language, in a different country, and with culturally different clients. Would I keep on failing myself and the client? I believe that the size of the consulting room is a good metaphor for how I had felt in the first months in the UK.

. . . with different field conditions

In theory, Parlett (2000) lists self-recognition as one of the five abilities of creative adjustment in a changing world. He sees these abilities as functions of and by the surrounded field rather than as a function of the individual alone. In practical terms "I became a bit of a stranger to myself" (Appel-Opper, 2007, p. 36). For some, like Özbek and Wohlfahrt (2006) and Parlett (2000), migration means a disruption of the self. From a dialogical gestalt perspective, Wheeler (2005) lists some propositions such as "additional supports" (p. 59) for "this difficult field" of intercultural work ". . . in which we get to know our own culture only in the encounter with another culture" (p. 45).

My fantasy is that I would have continued to fail. I felt stranded, downsized, but my supervision made a difference. These sessions actually provided me with this additional support: a space in which I felt safe to air my experiences and my frustrations. The frustration also entered the group supervisory sessions as my colleagues at first did not understand what I was trying to say. Seeing the puzzled facial expressions of my colleagues, again and again, added to the frustration of not having my linguistic power as in my first language. It was wonderful that my supervisor transferred what I had said into common parlance and how my colleagues then understood. I suppose that she herself, having emigrated to the UK from another country, must have experienced entering another culture at a professional and private level.

"When you are ready, the clients will come!"

This was a comment I kept on hearing from one of the supervision colleagues. Slowly I became ready, my private practice started to develop.

I recall another client, a fifty-year-old man, out of breath, beginning to speak as soon as we started to move upstairs to the room I had booked for this session. He spoke very fast, it was challenging for my German ears to follow what he was saying. I could sit there nodding and pretending to understand him or I could ask, thus interrupting him and in a way "taking over". Revisiting this scene, it felt like a no-win situation. As soon as I interrupted him, my German accent entered the room, my otherness was audible. I remember how he looked at me, and then sharing that he was an Irish man living in the UK.

There were many scenes like that, in which my otherness was out there (e.g., Appel-Opper, 2007). Over time I learnt to work with this. I learnt to use British humour. I developed different interventions. I would ask: "If we were in your country, what would a therapist from your culture say to this?" I would bring in the first language in asking whether the client could repeat this in her/his first language. I would say: "If we were in Germany, I would ask you about your sexuality. Good that we are not in Germany."

In the UK, I worked with clients, supervisees, and trainees who were racially and culturally different from me. It was interesting how we found each other. Many told me how important it was for them that I was not English, adding that they felt more free to share their experiences with "the English" with me. I remember stories about how their parents, immigrating from a different country, found a way into English culture, and how painful this had been. And what that had meant for them as the children of these parents. During these years of working in a second language, I continued to develop my work from what I have called a Living Body perspective. Paying attention to the non-verbal behaviour, how the body communicates, enriched my intercultural work (see Appel-Opper, 2012).

I recall the work with a female black supervisee. She mentioned her emotional impact about the fact that her grandparents had moved back to Jamaica. I then asked her whether she wanted to tell me more about Jamaica. I recall how we both spoke about our homes far away from our British homes and what she and I sometimes missed living in the UK. As we ended our supervisory relationship she told me how she especially valued this session. She added that she felt that her Jamaican roots were welcomed in our sessions. This was not the case with my clients when I started to work as a psychotherapist back in Germany. This feels like a loss.

Re-entering another intercultural field—coming home failing—failing to come home

An opportunity arose to take us back to Germany. What were we to do? In the end, I knew that I had to go back. I had to come back to my first language, to my first culture, to face my old wounds.

Mind the gap

When I first returned I took to my bicycle rather than a car. At times it felt as if my body wanted to fill the gap of twelve years in which I did not live in Germany. I inhaled smells and heard sounds that I had not perceived for a long time. Memories of my childhood and of my life before I left Germany reached me more easily.

Due to new legislation, my old German qualifications were not valid anymore, and my recent qualification as a UKCP registered psychotherapist was not accepted in Germany. So, as in the UK before, I went through a process of accreditation, this time as "Psychological Psychotherapist", qualifying to buy a licensed practice for which German health insurance companies pay for the therapy offered when applicable and granted. The main criterion to successfully buy a practice is the date of the accreditation. With a date as a beginner I had low chances to buy a practice. Unlike my colleagues who had grown into this system, I had to fill another gap. I left an established practice in the UK, entering in what felt like a grey zone in which I was not sure about how I could work in this new system. My practice was a non-starter. The project of coming home failed and I felt stranded again.

At this time, I offered international seminars on cultural awareness. I remember an exercise from a seminar in Norway. I asked the participants to imagine ET—an alien from another planet—ringing their door bells, asking them to tell him everything he should know about Norwegian culture. I enjoyed seeing how the colleagues were engaged in the exercise. At the end of a lively discussion, a participant said that she did not believe how complicated it would be to be a Norwegian. She added that this seemed impossible to learn and: "how must foreigners struggle".

Sometimes in these years I felt as being no longer British and no more/not yet German. Was I ET now? Yes and no. I wanted to belong, both at a personal and a professional level. I relived a scene from my childhood: a young girl running home, wanting to tell her experiences. At times, I ran to the wrong places, which made me feel unwelcomed and unwanted. As in the UK, I needed and found additional support, this time also in my own psychotherapeutic sessions. I lived through these enactments and co-creations, processing how I had felt "othered" in my family of origin.

At the seminar, I introduced myself as somebody who lived in various countries and returned to Germany as a matter of fact. I believe that I felt a bit like ET: an outsider who might be able to genuinely question some of the unspoken cultural presuppositions and who at the same time was not sure about her own place any more.

In the break, however, I sat next to a colleague who asked me about my experiences of coming back to Germany. She told me that she herself lived for some years abroad and added how very challenging it was for her to return to her own country.

The first client . . .

The phone rang, a woman asking for psychotherapy. As money was tight for her, I offered her a low fee. From my work in the UK I got used to the custom of working with a sliding scale, enabling clients with very low income to afford psychotherapy. We saw each other for about eight months. We focused on her upbringing in the old GDR—the former East Germany—and how to understand her patterns of obeying, staying invisible, and not trusting herself within this cultural field. However, it seemed as if we came close to a wall within our work. We were two stranded women, who lost a lot. It seemed as if she could only grow as big as I was at this time. After about seven months, she told me that she preferred not to come to the next session, but in two weeks, "as I cannot afford it." I wished I had challenged the both of us in what that communicated about our process. Did she feel guilty or ashamed that she paid such a small sum? At this time I could not. It felt as if I could not access the strengths and resources I had when I worked in the UK. I let her slip away more and more. I wonder whether by paying so little, she might not have felt herself entitled to criticise or wanting more from these sessions. In the last session she said that the therapy helped her. She added that she started to look for a new job, and that the ongoing discounting behaviour of her boss was not acceptable any more. My hunch now is that we gave each other crutches. For me, I realised that I did not lose all of my ability as a therapist and for her, I suppose she felt valued that a woman who came from the outside world (she never travelled herself and had dreams about this) sat, listened, and tried to be of help to her.

. . . and a German therapist in Germany: who now starts to express the difference?

Dhillons-Stevens (2004) sees self-disclosure as necessary in working with—in her case—racial difference. Similar to her, I ask: how should the question of race and culture be brought into the room?

I was accepted by an EAP (Employee Assistance Program) provider who already referred clients to me in the UK. I remember a client whose parents migrated from Palestine, first to Britain and then to Berlin. When I revisit this first session, I notice that she sat straight up in the chair, trying hard to tell me all I needed to know to help her. I recall that I told her how I over-adapted when I lived and worked in the UK. She immediately replied how hard she tried to blend into German culture and how painful her experiences had been, especially at her work. In the following sessions we focused on scenes of discrimination and racism. This helped her to get more into contact with her anger and the rage that seemed to be held in her neck and in her back. A few months after the therapy finished, she e-mailed to say that one of my embodied interventions, me throwing cushions and her watching me, stayed with her. She added that she started to realise how, from an early age, she displayed to her parents that everything was fine with her despite her frustrating experiences of living in the UK and then in Germany. I might have failed this client. Was it a good idea to bring in my own migrant experiences? How could my experiences be close to hers? Unlike her, I was able to dim my (cultural) difference, while her (racial) difference stayed visible. I also could have reduced her just to her cultural identity and not seen her individuality.

When I worked in the UK my own migration background was noticeable, audible through my German accent. With my move to Berlin, my field conditions have changed again. Speaking English with a German accent in Germany is not different any more. Who will I become now? Will I stay a bit like ET? Similar to my work in Britain, more and more non-German English speaking clients have found me. Are those clients attracted as they might be predisposed to be discounted, not acknowledged in the complexities of their cultural identity? In the last years I have seen more migrant clients who seem to live in a cupboard, online with the world of social media but with no real relationships with people where they live. Are they staying forever ET, travelling the world, staying some years there and then moving on to another language and culture, carrying their ambivalent, unresolved attachment patterns from their childhood? Do we fail them? With every different country they live in, the "graves of language" (Tömmel, 2010, p. 98) are becoming harder to reach. My heart goes out to them.

Acknowledgement

I want to thank Sabine Bird, Maria Gilbert, Philippa Perry, Annedore Prengel, Cynthia Ransley, and my husband for all their help and encouragement.

CHAPTER FIFTEEN

Losing my religion? Psychotherapeutic practice as repetition compulsion of character rigidity

Asaf Rolef Ben-Shahar

Is it ok to like myself?

At thirteen, nearing my Bar-Mitzvah, my father woke me up early, telling me there was no school today. I later learned that my cousin was killed that evening, during the last few weeks of his mandatory military service. Hit by an RPG rocket, he died immediately. At the grave, a full military ceremony was given. Many people spoke and prayed; many cried.

It feels so unreal, so formal, everybody is wearing uniforms. My father, uncle, and grandfather all cry. I have never seen either of them cry before. Lost and out of place, I stand at the edge of the crowd, eating rosemary leaves from a bush that decorates one of the graves. I cannot feel a thing, neither sadness, nor fear, nor anger; not a thing. I am certain that I am broken, completely inhuman. Everybody else seems to feel so intensely, and I suddenly become fearful that people would notice I did not belong there, with humankind; that this deep and dark secret about me would be revealed. Discreetly I wet my pinkie finger and apply some fake tears to my eyes, to at least appear human.

The gap between inside and outside has forever haunted me, but I have come to accept that mirrors do not reflect how I look, but instead provide a snapshot of self-experiencing. How great it would have been to consistently look at myself more kindly. In my mind, it relates to a recurring experience from my early years: I am a toddler, looking in the mirror and pulling faces, smiling to myself and talking. My mother steps in the room and says in a scolding tone: "you really do like yourself, don't you."

In instigating this book, I was hoping to shed particular light on failure within relational conceptualisation and understanding, where humanity, mutuality, self-disclosure, and the therapist's subjectivity were exceptionally exposed. Since the phenomenology of failure is, for me, intertwined with shame, I wanted to hear how other therapists worked through the shame of what they perceived as failure.

Yet last year has been personally and spiritually stormy for me—for the first time in my adult life I began to question some previously untouched personal, professional, and spiritual choices. "You have shuffled all your cards at the same time," my supervisor noted. Truthfully? It does not feel fully in my control. I am flooded with visions and channelling information that clash with my cognitive beliefs. I have no choice except to receive it, and let it in. I feel lost and open, hurting and loving. I have never experienced so much openness, so much suffering and love in my life. When asked how I am, I mostly do not know how to answer—a new position for me; scary, and blessed.

With so much change in my personal life, I felt obliged to take a sabbatical leave from doing psychotherapy, hoping to integrate the spiritual material into my work, wishing to centre my being around my personal rather than my professional life. I question some of the prices I have paid over the years for my choice to work as a psychotherapist. Specifically, I attempt to look at how some of aspects of my shame were perpetuated by my successful practice: putting myself second, attending to other people's needs before even noticing mine. I wish to speak of my own shame failure and the role psychotherapy played in it. This is a personal account, yet it may also resonate with others. I ask you to read it with kind eyes and kind heart if you can.

Is it ok to take space?

Can I take space without feeling shame? Can I like myself as I take space? It would be nice to spend time looking in the mirror again, pulling faces and liking this man reflected there, in the mirror. I want my own words to be heard, my own views and beliefs, values and creative expressions listened to. I can do this by writing, and in teaching. But daring to take space within psychotherapy is a different story. After all, clients pay us to centre our attention on them, on their difficulties, hopes, and fears.

Relational psychoanalysis and psychotherapy softened the shame connected with the desire to take space, by conceptualising mutuality and attachment (and even love) as central therapeutic axes (Aron, 1996; Mitchell, 2000), and valuing appropriate self-disclosure (B. Pizer, 2006; Rachman, 2001; Slavin, 2013; Ziv-Beiman, 2013) as relevant, and sometimes essential for the therapeutic relationship, and therapeutic progress. Relational theory has allowed for the subjectivity of the analyst to safely reside within the therapeutic dyad, yet by allowing this, it has also provided a potentially collusive sublimation for the therapist's narcissistic needs. I can now take space as a therapist without feeling so ashamed; such a stance could be justified with substantial theoretical grounding. But within this conceptualisation my subjectivity is still at the service of the therapeutic process and the client. The therapist's subjectivity does not stand in and by itself. I am therefore in danger of misusing theory to justify my need to be seen, thus implicitly labelling the desire to be seen and take space as innately requiring justification (and therefore innately questionable). The act of granting self-disclosure a stamp of theoretical approval also shames the desire for it.

Clearly, the therapeutic setting is not meant for the therapist's self-expression. Therapy is based on the characterological traits that keep the therapist's pathological, as well as healthy, narcissism in check, ensuring he or she would retain their "narcissistic disturbance" (as Alice Miller (1981) described it), or their "internal tug to respond" (a somewhat kinder conceptualisation of Stuart Pizer (2012)); that guilt would be attached to any self-centredness of the clinician.

Is there a doctor on the plane?

Coming back from teaching a seminar in Europe, I am seated in my chair on a night flight, trying to sleep. Suddenly all the lights are turned on; a loud commotion. "Is there a doctor on the flight?" My heart is pounding. "He is having a heart attack," shouts the stewardess.

"Is there a doctor on the plane?"

Should I get up? Should I? I am not medically trained. Surely there is a doctor on the plane? But, I think, sometimes panic attacks resemble heart attacks. Perhaps this is psychological, in which case I could be of use; should I not check? Is it responsible to simply remain seated? But I always involve myself in these situations. I want to do something differently and remain seated. My mind is restless, though. I make a deal with myself: I willl check if the man is attended to. If not I will get up. When the stewardess passes by I ask, "Did you find a doctor?" she nods.

In theory, now is the time to recline the chair and go back to sleep. However, I spend the remaining time of the flight struggling to let go of fact that I did not get up, and oscillating between being happy that I did not and feeling guilty for it.

I wonder if all the people on that night flight were as preoccupied with the question of getting up and providing some sort of help to this man. Would it have been different had the airplane been full of psychotherapists?

There is an inherent paradox to psychotherapeutic work. We position ourselves at the service of the other—reflecting them to themselves, offering ourselves as containers for their pain, surviving ourselves and them. This is a very complex act, requiring external attunement (Field, 1985; Knoblauch, 2011), resonance, and empathic capacities (Kohut, 1959; Preston & de Waal, 2002). But the very sensitivity that fosters the therapeutic act also makes us vulnerable, prone to introjection of suffering, to over-identifying, to taking too much in (Rolef Ben-Shahar, 2013, 2014). At the heart of what enables us to become good therapists, and alongside the healing our practice offers others and ourselves, lies a harmful potential, a risk for repetition compulsion of self-abandonment.

The wounded healer's remedy

I want to hold the boy that I was in my cousin's memorial service, and the man who preoccupied himself with the hurting man on a plane, and offer them some solace. In my hurting and confused place I am trying to find whether it is feasible to heal the wounds that I carry as a person while remaining in practice. I have yet to find an answer. What happens when most of my working week is dedicated to the very same practice that shaped my deepest wounds? Perhaps this is a paper about losing my religion; and at this time it is written with little knowing or certainty.

Sociologist Eva Illouz (2008) argued that psychological culture tended to perpetuate societal stagnation by pacifying righteous aggressive and transformative impulses. Over-analysis, says Illouz, prevents us from responding to social injustices. She believes that psychology inadvertently serves the interest of capitalist, organisational, and financial structures, and not necessarily the interests of the people. Perhaps her claims are extreme, but could the value of psychotherapy correspond to the potential stagnation it encourages? In wanting to do good, might we sometimes create stagnation and impotence? Could it be that this is also true for us? That the very act of practicing psychotherapy takes a grave toll from us therapists—not just when working with severe traumas, which is widely researched (Figley, 1995; Hadad & Rolef Ben-Shahar, 2012; Mac Ian & Pearlman, 1990; Rothschild & Rand, 2006). Following Illouz's (2008) line of thought, perhaps the narcissistic pathology of psychotherapists serves society and is thus rarely touched on; maybe it is against the interest of psychological organisations to attend to this wound. Perhaps we should at times protest against becoming psychotherapists? That sometimes, instead of making lemonade from lemons, we should look for another tree?

That most of us begin working from our biographical wound is pretty much agreed on, particularly in relational thinking. Winnicott (1963), concurring with Jung, asserted "only the wounded healers heal" (p. 134). But what about those wounds, though? Is it possible to work through such wounds when we continuously expose ourselves to their affect—like peeling a scab without allowing its organismic course of healing to unfold? Have you managed? And if I did allow it appropriate time and a sociologically-informed consideration, would I still choose to practice psychotherapy? Am I even allowed to engage with this heresy? And moreover, who would I be if I was not a psychotherapist? Can I just be me?

Everybody is entitled to their suffering

I wish to look at some of the characteristics that made me and my work so suited for one another, and therefore so challenging. Perhaps I am not that special, and some other psychotherapists share similar characteristics. From a very young age, I noticed others before it was possible to attend to myself. I noticed others' needs and emotions, frequently before these were expressed. External attunement is characteristic of preoccupied attachment style (Main, 2000), and is found in many highly sensitive children (E. Aron, 2003; Miller, 1981, 1995). This attunement makes it possible to extend our antennae and notice things before they are spoken (Field, 1985; Knoblauch, 2011; Lewis et al., 2000). As a child, I considered my mum's physical and psychological well-being as much more central and important than my own.

Another quality concerns the drive to respond, to act, which Alice Miller (1981) called *narcissistic disturbance*, and Stuart Pizer termed *an internal tug to respond* (2012). Not only are we externally attuned but we are also strongly affected by what we notice. Psychotherapists tend to find it harder than most people to witness someone else's suffering. It does not necessarily mean that we actually do something about it, but that regardless of whether we do or do not respond, we feel a strong tug to it. I imagine that most passengers on the plane were able to go back to sleep once the man was medically attended to.

The amplified impulse to reach out and respond to another person's distress makes our lives quite tense (since there is always suffering), but I would like to believe that the world would have been less friendly if nobody felt "an internal tug to respond" to other people's suffering. The willingness to be moved also results in our investing in connection, in healing, in bringing about change. Stuart Pizer (2012) acknowledges the narcissistic aspects of this "tug to respond" but also considers it a part of the therapist's generous involvement: willingness to give of herself and be responsive to the other. Generosity, unlike reactivity, implies choice, and it is this choice that I am questioning here. In Antonio Damasio's (1994) somatic markers theory, he suggests that empathic listeners unconsciously emulate physiological postures, muscular holdings, and contractions to attempt and understand the other "from within". If we make the ingestion of other people's emotions our business, what is it that we are exposing ourselves to? Is there a genuine choice involved, a true mindful position? Or are we—am I—accepting how we were born and raised, and are attempting to make the best of it; and back with the lemonade.

I try to remember that everybody is entitled to their suffering, that I have no right to take someone's suffering from them. That, in fact, I cannot.

The last characteristic I wish to speak of is our narcissistic belief that we can actually do something about someone else's pain; that we have the power to help: if we only listen for long enough, or if we prescribe the right medication, or if we offer the right interpretation/intervention at the right time, then we can help and reorganise, or change, or heal, or at least reduce (depending on your orientation) the suffering of the other. This belief is not only a psychological stance—it is a spiritual positioning of faith and agency, and one that is arguably necessary to hold alongside a more realistic and calculative stance. It also has some truth in it, but it feels important to also acknowledge here the fallacy of this assumption.

As I turn this scrutiny inwards, I have to admit, not without shame, that a great deal of my sense of worth actually stems from helping others. A long therapeutic day makes it easier for me to walk in the world; it is easier for me to be myself when I have made a benevolent impact on another person. And now? My sabbatical churns and challenges my right to be here on this earth, it hurts to feel how much I need to be of use. I am confronted by my belief that I have to give to the other in order to feel meaningful. Do I have to support someone else to sense my worth? For the first time in my life I want to ask—is this practice of being helpful for others doing me good? Is it healthy for me? Is it healing for me? Does it make me happy?

Losing my religion?

What shall I do without this religion? Is it possible to practice therapy with a deep uncertainty about its very essence? Practicing psychotherapy is what I do best. From birth I was trained and raised to become a therapist. I love my therapeutic practice, but it is also very dangerous for me. Over the years I learned better self-care, but in essence I failed in taking care of myself as I would have liked. I am still ashamed of wanting to look in the mirror, of wanting to like myself in the mirror. Sometimes I am still uncertain about my right to belong to the esteemed club of humanity. This is my biggest therapeutic failure, and one that undoubtedly has impacted my clinical ability—I could not embody a state of "unconditional being". Just like my cousin's service, at times psychotherapy granted me a few fake (or real) tears to qualify my right to be a person.

But what can I do? I developed my entire skill base around helping other people. I learned to be more attentive, to self-regulate as
means for dyadic regulation, to watch my need for fixing and to allow
the other space. I can practice for thirty hours a week and more, a
production line of benevolent analysis, help and support. I can
endure. Moreover, I really do like myself when I practice; I become
alive during therapeutic connections, but it makes me deeply dependent on my body of practice. Can I sense my vitality in my personal,
relational, sexual life without qualifications, without justifications? I
am fearful, terrified even, that my searching acts of heresy will end up
with me returning to practice with my tail between my legs; that I
would practice psychotherapy not out of choice, but in par with my
character. That, to borrow Elad Hadad's (this volume) perspective, I
shall give up the impulse to rebel against professional deadening, and
return to be of service. Is it possible, however, to choose differently?
Is it possible for me to transcend this binary position and practice with
commitment to self-kindness? I truly hope so; I do not wish to dutifully pray to the god of psychotherapy anymore; but I would certainly
like to bring my own spiritual beliefs and join in with others, to make
my personal rather than my professional self the centre of my life, and
still be welcomed in this community.

REFERENCES

Adler, A. (1928). Psychologie und Medizin. *Wiener medizinische Wochenschrift, 78*: 697–700.

Andreas, C., & Andreas, T. (1991). Aligning perceptual positions. *A New Distinction in NLP. Anchor Point, 5*(2): 1–6.

Appel-Opper, J. (2007). Intercultural communication: my own personal journey through culture. *British Journal of Psychotherapy Integration, 3*(1): 36–41.

Appel-Opper, J. (2012). Intercultural body-oriented psychotherapy: the culture in the body and the body in the culture. In: C. Young (Ed.), *About Relational Body Psychotherapy* (pp. 201–216). Stow: Body Psychotherapy.

Arntz, A., Klokman, J., & Sieswerda, S. (2005). An experimental test of the schema mode model of borderline personality disorder. *Journal of Behavior Therapy and Experimental Psychiatry, 36*(3): 226–239.

Aron, E. N. (2003). *The Highly Sensitive Child: Helping Our Children Thrive When the World Overwhelms Them*. London: Thorsons.

Aron, L. (1996). *A Meeting of Minds: Mutuality in Psychoanalysis*. Hillsdale, NJ: Analytic Press.

Aron, L. (1997). Are we to have a meeting of minds? *Psychoanalytic Dialogues, 7*: 885–896.

Aron, L., & Starr, K. (2013). *A Psychotherapy for the People: Towards a Progressive Psychoanalysis*. Hove: Routledge.

Asheri, S. (2004). Erotic desire in the therapy room. Dare we embody it? Can we afford not to? Paper presented at the 2004 UKCP conference, London. Retrieved from: www.yobeely.f2s.com/articles/eroticdesire.html

Atwood, G. (2011). *The Abyss of Madness*. New York: Routledge.

Bamelis, L., Giesen-Bloo, J., Bernstein, D., & Arntz, A. (2012). Effectiveness studies of schema therapy. In: M. Vreeswijk, J. Broersen, & M. Nadort (Eds.), *The Wiley-Blackwell Handbook of Schema Therapy: Theory, Research and Practice* (pp. 495–510). New York: Wiley.

Bandura, A. (1989). Human agency in social cognitive theory. *American Psychologist, 44*: 1175–1184.

Bandura, A. (2006). Toward a psychology of human agency. *Perspectives on Psychological Science, 1*: 164–180.

Bass, A., & Moss, D. (2012). On keeping thought erotic: some problems in contemporary theory and practice. *Division/Review*: 29–33.

Beck, U. (1992). *Risk Society: Towards a New Modernity*. London: Sage.

Beebe, B., & Lachmann, F. (2002). *Infant Research and Adult Treatment*. Hillsdale, NJ: Analytic Press.

Behary, T. W. (2013). *Disarming the Narcissist* (2nd edn). Oakland, CA: New Harbinger.

Benjamin, J. (2004). Beyond doer and done to: an intersubjective view of thirdness. *Pyschoanalytic Quarterly, 63*: 5–46.

Benjamin, J. (2009). A relational psychoanalysis perspective on the necessity of acknowledging failure in order to restore the facilitating and containing features of the intersubjective relationship (the shared third). *International Journal of Psychoanalysis, 90*: 441–445.

Bloom, S. L. (2006). Neither liberty nor safety: the impact of fear on individuals, institutions, and society, Part IV. *Psychotherapy and Politics International, 4*(1): 4–23.

Boadella, D. (2011). Psycho-physical synthesis at the foundations of body psychotherapy: the 100-year legacy of Pierre Janet (1859–1947). In: C. Young (Ed.), *The Historical Basis of Body Psychotherapy* (pp. 49–66). Stow: Body Psychotherapy.

Bohleber, W., Fonagy, P., Jiménez, J. P., Scarfone, D., Varvin, S., & Zysman, S. (2013). Towards a better use of psychoanalytic concepts: a model illustrated using the concept of enactment. *International Journal of Psycho-Analysis, 94*: 501–530.

Bollas, C. H. (1986). *The Shadow of the Object: Psychoanalysis of the Unthought Known*. London: Free Association.

Boyesen, G. (Ed.). (1980). *Collected Papers on Biodynamic Psychology*. London: Biodynamic Psychology.

Bromberg, P. M. (1991). On knowing one's patient inside out: the aesthetics of unconscious communication. *Psychoanalytic Dialogues, 1*: 399–422.

Bromberg, P. M. (1996). Standing in the spaces: the multiplicity of self and the psychoanalytic relationship. *Contemporary Psychoanalysis, 32*: 509–535.

Bromberg, P. M. (1998). *Standing in the Spaces: Essays on Clinical Process, Trauma, and Dissociation*. Hillsdale, NJ: Analytic Press.

Bromberg, P. M. (2006). *Awakening the Dreamer: Clinical Journeys*. Mawah, NJ: Analytic Press.

Bromberg, P. M. (2011). *The Shadow of the Tsunami*. New York: Routledge.

Brothers, D. (2008). *Toward a Psychology of Uncertainty: Trauma-Centered Psychoanalysis*. New York: Analytic Press.

Brothers, D. & Lewinberg, E. (1999). The therapeutic partnership. In: A. Goldberg (Ed.), *Progress in Self Psychology, Vol. 5* (pp. 259–284). Hillsdale, NJ: Analytic Press.

Chodron, P. (1997). *When Things Fall Apart*. Boston, MA: Shambala.

Cornell, W. (2009). An eruption of erotic vitality between a male analyst and a male patient. In: B. Reis & R. Grossmark (Eds.), *Heterosexual Masculinities: Contemporary Perspectives from Psychoanalytic Gender Theory* (pp. 127–150). New York: Routledge.

Damasio, A. (1994). *Descartes' Error: Emotion, Reason, and the Human Brain*. New York: Penguin.

Davies, J. M. (2004). Whose bad objects are we anyway? Repetition and our elusive love affair with evil. *Psychoanalytic Dialogues, 14*: 711–732.

Dhillon-Stevens, H. (2004). Personal and professional integration of anti-oppressive practice and the multiple oppression model in psychotherapeutic education. *The British Journal Of Psychotherapy Integration: The Exploration Continues, 1*(2): 47–59.

Dhillon-Stevens, H. (2012). Clinical applications of working with race, culture and ethicity. In: C. Feltham & I. Horton (Eds.), *The SAGE Handbook of Counselling and Psychotherapy* (pp. 641–649). London: SAGE.

Dimen, M. (1994). Money, love, and hate: contradiction and paradox in psychoanalysis. *Psychoanalytic Dialogues, 1*: 69–100.

Dimen, M. (2003). *Sexuality, Intimacy, Power*. Hillsdale, NJ: Analytic Press.

Dimen, M., & Amrhein, C. (forthcoming). Eight topics: a conversation on sexual boundary violations. In: J. Alpert & A. L. Steinberg (Eds.).

160   REFERENCES

Epstein, S. (2013). War is a crying thing. *Somatic Psychotherapy Today, 3*: 36–42.

Feldenkrais, M. (1977). *Awareness through Movement: Health Exercises for Personal Growth*. Harmondsworth: Penguin.

Ferenczi, S. (1933). Confusion of tongues between adults and the child. In: *Final Contributions to the Problems and Methods of Psychoanalysis* (pp. 156–167). London: Karnac, 1980.

Ferenczi, S. (1980). *Further Contributions to the Theory and Technique of Psycho-Analysis*, J. Richman (Ed.), J. Suttie (Trans.). London: Karnac.

Field, T. (1985). Attachment as psychobiological attunement: being on the same wavelength. In: M. Reite & T. Field (Eds.), *The Psychobiology of Attachment and Separation* (pp. 415–454). Orlando, FL: Academic Press.

Figley, C. R. (1995). Compassion fatigue as secondary traumatic stress disorder: an overview. In: C. R. Figley (Ed.), *Compassion Fatigue: Coping with Secondary Traumatic Stress Disorder in Those who Treat the Traumatized* (pp. 1–20). New York: Brunner/Mazel.

Fonagy, P. (2002). Welcome to the Profession. Graduation Talk, The Bowlby Centre, London, July 2002.

Freud, S. (1891). Hypnosis. *S. E., 1*: 103–114. London: Hogarth.

Freud, S. (1912e). Recommendations to physicians practising psycho-analysis. *S.E., 12*: 109–120. London: Hogarth.

Freud, S. (1920g). *Beyond the Pleasure Principle. S.E., 18*: 7–64 London: Hogarth.

Freud, S. (1937c). *Analysis terminable and interminable. S. E., 23*: 211–253. London: Hogarth.

Ghent, E. (1990). Masochism, submission, surrender. *Contemporary Psychoanalysis, 26*: 169–211.

Gilbert, C. (1999). Breathing: the legacy of Wilhelm Reich. *Journal of Bodywork & Movement Therapies, 3*(2): 97–106.

Goldberg, A. (2012). *The Analysis of Failure*. Hove: Routledge.

Greif, D., & Livingston, R. H. (2013). An interview with Philip M. Bromberg PhD. *Contemporary Psychoanalysis, 49*: 323–355.

Hadad, E., & Rolef Ben-Shahar, A. (2012). The things we're taking home with us: understanding therapist's self-care in trauma work. *International Journal of Psychotherapy, 16*(1): 50–61.

Hill, S. (2008). Language and intersubjectivity: multiplicity in a bilingual treatment. *Psychoanalytic Dialogues, 18*: 437–455.

Hirsch, I. (1993). Countertransference enactments and some issues related to external factors in the analyst's life. *Psychoanalytic Dialogues, 3*: 343–366.

Hoffman, I. Z. (1998). *Ritual and Spontaneity in the Psychoanalytic Process: A Dialectical-Constructionist View*. Hillsdale, NJ: Analytic Press.

Illouz, E. (2008). *Saving the Modern Soul: Therapy, Emotions, and the Culture of Self-Help*. Berkeley, CA: University of California Press.

Keleman, S. (1981). *Your Body Speaks its Mind*. Berkeley, CA: Center Press.

Keleman, S. (1990). *Körperlicher Dialog in der therapeutischen Beziehung*. Munich: Kösel.

Keleman, S. (2012). Forming an embodied life: the difference between being bodied and forming an embodied life. *International Body Psychotherapy Journal, 11*(1): 51–56.

King, A. (2011). Touch as relational affirmation. *Attachment: New Directions in Psychotherapy and Relational Psychoanalysis, 5*: 108–124.

Kipling, R. (1910). If—. In: *Rewards and Faries*. Garden City, NY: Doubleday Page.

Knoblauch, S. (2011). Contextualizing attunement within the polyrhythmic weave: the psychoanalytic samba. *Psychoanalytic Dialogues, 21*(4): 414–427.

Kogan, I. (2007). *The struggle against mourning*. Lanham, MD: Jason Aronson.

Kohut, H. (1959). Introspection, empathy, and psychoanalysis—an examination of the relationship between mode of observation and theory. *Journal of the American Psychoanalytic Association, 7*: 459–483.

Kottler, J. A., & Carlson, J. (2003). *Bad Therapy: Master Therapists Share their Worst Failures*. New York: Brunner-Routledge.

Levenson, E. A. (1983). *The Ambiguity of Change: An Inquiry Into the Nature of Psychoanalytic Reality*. New York: Basic.

Levenson, E. A. (1995). *The Fallacy of Understanding: An Inquiry Into the Changing Structure of Psychoanalysis*. Northvale, NJ; London: J. Aronson.

Levine, P. A. (2005). Panic, biology and reason: giving the body its due. In: N. Totton (Ed.), *New Dimensions in Body Psychotherapy* (pp. 30-39). Maidenhead: Open University.

Levine, P. A., & Frederick, A. (1997). *Waking the Tiger*. Berkley, CA: North Atlantic Books.

Levy, R. (2013). Relational body psychotherapy as a transpersonal encounter: mutual surrender. *Hebrew Psychology*. Retrieved from: www.hebpsy.net/articles.asp?t=0&id=3002

Lewis, T., Amini, F., & Lannon, R. (2000). *A General Theory of Love*. New York: Random House.

Little, M. I. (1977). *Psychotic Anxieties and Containment: A Personal Record of an Analysis with Winnicott*. Northvale, NJ: Jason Aronson.

Lobban, G. (2013). The immigrant analyst: a journey from double consciousness toward hybridity. *Psychoanalytic Dialogues, 23*: 554–567.

Loewald, H. (1980). *Papers on Psychoanalysis*. New Haven, CT: Yale University Press.

Mac Ian, P. S., & Pearlman, L. A. (1990). Vicarious traumatization: a framework for understanding the psychological effects of working with victims. *Journal of Traumatic Stress, 3*: 131–149.

Main, M. (2000). The organized categories of infant, child, and adult attachment: flexible *vs.* inflexible attention under attachment-related stress. *Journal of the American Psychoanalytic Association, 48*: 1055–1095.

Masson, J. F. (1985). *The Assault on Truth*. New York: Penguin.

Merleau-Ponty, M. (1966). *Phänomenologie der Wahrnehmung*. Berlin: De Gruyter.

Messler Davies, J. (2003). Falling in love with love: oedipal and postoedipal manifestations of idealization, mourning, and erotic masochism. *Psychoanalytic Dialogues, 13*: 1–27.

Miller, A. (1981). *The Drama of the Gifted Child*. New York: Basic Books.

Miller, A. (1995). *The Drama of Being a Child: The Search for the True Self* (revised edn). London: Virago.

Mitchell, S. A. (1993). *Hope and Dread in Psychoanalysis*. New York: Basic Books.

Mitchell, S. A. (1997). *Influence and Autonomy in Psychoanalysis*. Hillsdale, NJ: Analytic Press.

Mitchell, S. A. (2000). *Relationality: From Attachment to Intersubjectivity*. Hillsdale, NJ: Analytic Press.

Mitchell, S. A. (2005). *Influence and Autonomy in Psychoanalysis*. Hillsdale, NJ: Analytic Press.

Modell, A. H. (1984). On having the right to a life. In: *Psychoanalysis in a New Context* (pp. 55–69). New York: International University Press.

Morley, R. (2007). *The Analysand's Tale*. London: Karnac.

Muller, R. T. (2010). *Trauma and the Avoidant Client: Attachment-Based Strategies for Healing*. New York: Norton.

Murray, P. E., & Rotter, J. C. (2002). Creative counseling techniques for family therapists. *The Family Journal: Counselling and Therapy for Couples and Families, 10*(2): 203–206.

Ogden, T. (1989). *The Primitive Edge of Experience*. Northville, NJ: Aronson.

Ogden, T. (1992). The dialectically constituted/decentered subject of psychoanalysis (Parts I and II). *International Journal of Psychoanalysis, 73*: 517–526, 613–626.

Ogden, T. (1994a). *Subjects of Analysis*. Northvale, NJ: Aronson.

Ogden, T. (1994b). The analytic third: working with intersubjective clinical facts. *The International Journal of Psychoanalysis, 75*: 3–19.

Ogden, T. (2014). Fear of breakdown and the unlived life. *International Journal of Psychoanalysis, 95*(2): 205–223.

Özbek, T., & Wohlfahrt, E. (2006). Der transkulturelle Übergangsraum— ein Theorem und seine Funktion in der transkulturellen Psychotherapie am ZIPP [The cross-cultural transitional space—a theorem and its function in transcultural psychotherapy at ZIPP]. In: E. Wohlfahrt & M. Zaumseil (Eds.), *Transkulturelle Psychiatrie— Interkulturelle Psychotherapie: Interdisziplinäre Theorie und Praxis [Transcultural Psychiatry—Intercultural Psychotherapy: Interdisciplinary theory and practice]* (pp. 169–176). Heidelberg: Springer.

Parlett, M. (2000). Creative adjustment and the global field. *British Gestalt Journal, 9*(1): 15–27.

Partridge, S. (2014). The hidden neglect and sexual abuse of infant Sigmund Freud. *Attachment, 8*(2): 139–150.

Pizer, B. (1997). When the analyst is ill: dimensions of self-disclosure. *Psychoanalytic Quarterly, 66*: 450–469.

Pizer, B. (2003). When the crunch is a (k)not: a crimp in relational dialogue. *Psychoanalytic Dialogues, 13*: 171–192.

Pizer, B. (2005). Passion, responsibility, and "Wild Geese": creating a context for the absence of conscious intentions. *Psychoanalytic Dialogues, 15*: 57–84.

Pizer, B. (2006). Risk and potential in analytic disclosure: can the analyst make "the wrong thing" right? *Contemporary Psychoanalysis, 42*: 31–40.

Pizer, B. (2014). A clinical exploration of moving anger forward: intimacy, anger and creative freedom. *Psychoanalytic Dialogues, 24*(1): 14–28.

Pizer, S. A. (1992). The negotiation of paradox in the analytic process. *Psychoanalytic Dialogues, 2*: 215–240.

Pizer, S. A. (1998). *Building Bridges: The Negotiation of Paradox in Psychoanalysis*. Hillsdale, NJ: Analytic Press.

Pizer, S. A. (2000). A gift in return: the clinical use of writing about a patient. *Psychoanalytic Dialogues, 10*: 247–259.

Pizer, S. A. (2004). Impasse recollected in tranquility: love, dissociation, and discipline in the analytic process. *Psychoanalytic Dialogues, 14*: 289–311.

Pizer, S. A. (2012). The analyst's generous involvement: recognition and the tension of tenderness. Paper presented at the Affective relatedness and therapeutic action, The Relational training programme, Psychotherapy School at the Faculty of Medicine, Tel Aviv University.

Pizer, S. A. (2014). The analyst's generous involvement: recognition and the "tension of tenderness". *Psychoanalytic Dialogues, 24*: 1–13.

Pollock, L., & Slavin, J. (1998). The struggle for recognition: disruption and reintegration in the experience of agency. *Psychoanalytic Dialogues, 8*: 857–873.

Preston, S. D., & de Waal, F. B. M. (2002). Empathy: its ultimate and proximate bases. *Behavioral and Brain Sciences, 25*: 1–72.

Rachman, A. W. (2001). Beyond neutrality: the curative function of analyst self-disclosure. In: J. Reppen & J. Schulman (Eds.), *Way Beyond Freud: Post-Modern Conceptions of Psychoanalysis* (pp. 127–142). London: Opengate.

Racker, H. (1957). The meaning and uses of countertransference. *Psychoanalytic Quarterly, 26*: 303–357.

Racker, H. (1968). *Transference and Countertransference*. London: Karnac, 1982.

Rafaeli, E., Bernstein, D. P., & Young, J. (2011). *Schema Therapy: Distinctive Features*. New York: Routledge.

Rafaeli, E., Maurer, O., & Thoma, N. C. (2015). Working with modes in schema therapy. In: N. C. Thoma. & D. McKay (Eds.) *Working with Emotion in Cognitive-Behavioural Therapy* (pp. 263–287). New York: Guilford.

Reich, W. (1930). *The Sexual Revolution*, T. P. Wolfe (Trans.). New York: Octagon, 1971.

Reich, W. (1933). *The Mass Psychology of Fascism*. New York: Orgone Institute, 1946.

Reich, W. (1948). *The Discovery of the Orgone (Vol. 2): The Cancer Biopathy*. Kildonan: Banton, 1998.

Reich, W. (1951). *The Sexual Revolution: Toward a Self-Governing Character Structure*, T. P. Wolfe (Ed.) (3rd edn). London: P. Nevill; Vision P.

Reich, W. (1971). *Charakteranalyse*. Cologne: Kiepenheuer & Witsch.

Reich, W. (1973). *The Function of the Orgasm*, V. R. Carfagno (Trans.). London: Souvenir.

Rolef Ben-Shahar, A. (2007). Connecting in the age of accountability. *Self & Society, A Journal of Humanistic Psychology in Britain, 34*(4): 33–38.

Rolef Ben-Shahar, A. (2013). Fairy wings and the psychotherapeutic act: who's regulating whom. *Somatic Psychotherapy Today, 3*: 50–53.

Rolef Ben-Shahar, A. (2014). *Touching the Relational Edge–Body Psychotherapy*. London: Karnac.

Rothschild, B., & Rand, M. L. (2006). *Help for the Helper*: The *Psychophysiology of Compassion Fatigue and Vicarious Trauma*. New York: Norton.

Russell, P. L. (1996). Process with involvement: the interpretation of affect. In: L. E. Lifson (Ed.), *Understanding Therapeutic Action*: *Psychodynamic Concepts of Cure* (pp. 201–216). Hillsdale, NJ: Analytic Press.

Russell, P. L. (1998). Crises of emotional growth (a.k.a. theory of the crunch). Paper presented at the Paul Russell Conference, Boston, MA.

Russell, P. L. (2006a), The negotiation of affect. *Contemporary Psychoanalysis, 42*(4): 621–636.

Russell, P. L. (2006b). Trauma, repetition, and affect. *Contemporary Psychoanalysis, 42*(4): 601–620.

Samuels, A. (1993). *The Political Psyche*. London and New York: Routledge.

Samuels, A. (1996). From sexual misconduct to social justice. *Psychoanalytic Dialogues, 6*: 295–321.

Samuels, A. (2001). *Politics on the Couch*: *Citizenship and the Internal Life*. London: Profile.

Samuels, A. (2006). Psychotherapy on the couch? Psychotherapy and society—some possibilities and some limitations. In: N. Totton (Ed.), *The Politics of Psychotherapy, New Perspectives* (pp. 3–16). Maidenhead: Open University.

Samuels, A. (2015). *A New Therapy for Politics?* London: Karnac.

Sapriel, L., & Palumbo, D. (2001). Psyche and culture: an exercise in peer supervision. *British Gestalt Journal, 10*(2): 86–96.

Schore, A. N. (2003). *Affect Regulation & the Repair of the Self*. New York: Norton.

Schwartz, J. (1999). *Cassandra's Daughter*: *A History of Psychoanalysis in Europe and America*. London: Viking/Penguin [reissued London: Karnac, 2003].

Searles, H. F. (1979). The self in the countertransference. *Issues in Ego Psychology, 2*: 49–56.

Siegel, A. (1996). *Heinz Kohut and the Psychology of the Self*. New York: Routledge.

Slavin, J. (2012). It is all personal: further thoughts on therapeutic action: commentary on paper by Noelle Burton. *Psychoanalytic Dialogues, 22*: 679–686.

Slavin, J. (2013). Moments of truth and perverse scenarios in psycho-analysis: revisiting Davies' "Love in the afternoon". *Psychoanalytic Dialogues, 23*(2): 139–149.

Slavin, M., & Kriegman, D. (1998). Why the analyst needs to change. *Psychoanalytic Dialogues, 8*: 247–285.

Sperry, M. (2012). Sameness and difference: cultivating cultural dialogue *International Journal of Psychoanalytic Self-Psychology, 8*(1): 77–91.

Steiner, J. (1993). Problems of psychoanalytic technique: patient-centered and analyst-centered interpretations. In: *Psychic Retreats*. London: Routledge.

Steiner, J. (2006). Interpretative enactments and the analytic setting. *The International Journal of Psychoanalysis, 87*(2): 315–328.

Stern, D. B. (1983). Unformulated experience: from familiar chaos to creative disorder. *Contemporary Psychoanalysis, 19*: 71–99.

Stern, D. B. (1997). *Unformulated Experience: From Dissociation to Imagination in Psychoanalysis*. Hillsdale, NJ: Analytic Press.

Stern, D. B. (2004). The eye sees itself: dissociation, enactment, and the achievement of conflict. *Contemporary Psychoanalysis, 40*: 197–237.

Stern, D. B. (2010). *Partners in Thought: Working with Unformulated Experience, Dissociation, and Enactment*. New York: Routledge.

Stern, D. N. (2004). *The Present Moment in Psychotherapy and Everyday Life*. New York: Norton.

Sullivan, H. S. (1953). *The Interpersonal Theory of Psychiatry*. New York: Norton.

Tömmel, S. E. (2010). Culture-orientated psychoanalysis: on taking cultural back-ground into account in the therapy of migrants. In: A.-M. Schloesser & A. Gehrlach (Eds), *Crossing Borders—Integrating Differences. Psychoanalytic Psychotherapy in Transition* (pp. 95–112). London: Karnac.

Totton, N. (2000). *Psychotherapy and politics*. London: Sage.

Totton, N. (2006). The institutions of psychotherapy. In: N. Totton (Ed.), *The Politics of Psychotherapy, New Perspectives* (pp. 108–121). Maidenhead: Open University.

Totton, N., & Edmondson, E. (2009). *Reichian Growth Work: Melting the Blocks to Life and Love* (2nd edn). Ross-on-Wye: PCCS.

Tronick, E. (1989). Emotions and emotional communication in infants. *American Psychologist, 44*: 112–119.

Wachtel, P. L. (2014). An integrative relational point of view. *Psychotherapy, 51*(3): 342–349.

Walsh, S. D. (2014). The bilingual therapist and transference to language: language use in therapy and its relationship to object relational context. *Psychoanalytic Dialogues, 24*(1): 56–71.

Wenke, M. (2011). *Im Gehirn gibt es keine Gedanken. Bewusstsein und Wissenschaft* (2nd edn). Würzburg: Königshausen & Neumann.

Wheeler, G. (2005). Culture, self and field. In: T. Levine Bar-Yoseph (Ed.), *The Bridge: Dialogues Across Cultures* (pp. 27–50). Metairie/New Orleans: Gestalt Institute.

White, R. W. (1963). Ego and reality in psychoanalytic theory. In: *Psychological Issues*. Monograph 11. New York: International Universities Press.

Winnicott, C. (1980). Fear of breakdown: a clinical example. *International Journal of Psychoanalysis, 61*: 351–357.

Winnicott, D. W. (1960). The theory of the parent-infant relationship. In: *The Maturational Processes and the Facilitating Environment* (pp. 37–55). London: Karnac, 1990.

Winnicott, D. W. (1963). II. D.W.W.'s dream related to reviewing Jung. In: C. Winnicott, R. Shepherd, & M. Davis (Eds.), *Psycho-Analytic Explorations*. Cambridge, MA: Harvard University Press, 1989.

Winnicott, D. W. (1965).*The Maturational Process and the Facilitating Environment: Studies in the Theory of Emotional Development*. New York: International Universities Press.

Young, J. E., Klosko, J. S., & Weishaar, M. E. (2003). *Schema Therapy: A Practitioner's Guide*. New York: Guilford.

Ziv-Beiman, S. (2013). Therapist self-disclosure as an integrative intervention. *Journal of Psychotherapy Integration, 23*(1): 59–74.

INDEX